Real World
Parents

CHRISTIAN PARENTING FOR FAMILIES
LIVING IN THE REAL WORLD

MARK MATLOCK

ZONDERVAN®

ZONDERVAN.com/
AUTHORTRACKER
follow your favorite authors

youth
specialties

Dedication

How could I not take this opportunity to honor my own parents? If I can be half the parents they were, then my kids—Dax and Skye—will be fine. (I'm just worried about making it to "half"!) They aren't perfect, but they are authentic—and they live out the mission of Christ in the real world. They were my models for Real World Parents.

Mom and Dad, I love you.

Acknowledgments

A big thanks to everyone who helped Real World Parents journey over the last seven years.

David McDaniel, Mike Gwartney, Jonathan Matlock, David DeYoung, Bryan Kennedy, Alf Laukoter, Susie Lipps, Jim Thorpe, and David Welch all gave guidance and leadership at WisdomWorks during the formation of this vision.

Mark Oestreicher, Tic Long, and Jay Howver enabled me to keep Real World Parents alive. And, of course, the Youth Specialties staff actually kept the program going.

The content received many contributions along the way from talented people. Jim Hancock, Michael Novelli, Mark Novelli, Kelly Dolan at Imago Community, Dave Urbanski, and Chris Lyon impacted this book, providing direction as it changed over the years. I'm sure I took many of their ideas and never properly credited them for it. I am glad they're all my friends.

I also want to recognize the hundreds of Real World Presenters who teach the seminar in churches and communities throughout the country and around the world.

ZONDERVAN

Real World Parents: Christian Parenting for Families Living in the Real World
Copyright © 2010 by Mark Matlock

YS Youth Specialties is a trademark of YOUTHWORKS!, INCORPORATED and is registered with
the United Sates Patent and Trademark Office.

This title is also available as a Zondervan ebook.
Visit www.zondervan.com/ebooks.

Requests for information should be addressed to:
Zondervan, *Grand Rapids, Michigan 49530*

Library of Congress Cataloging-in-Publication Data

Matlock, Mark.
     Real world parents : Christian parenting for families living in the real
       world / Mark Matlock.
      p. cm.
     ISBN 978-0-310-66936-4 (pbk.)
      1. Parents—Religious life. 2. Parenting—Religious
aspects—Christianity. I. Title.
BV4529.M369 2010
248.8'45—dc22   2009044724

Interior design by Mark Novelli, IMAGO

Printed in the United States of America

10 11 12 13 14 15 • 24 23 22 21 20 19 18 17 16 15 14 13 12 11 10 9 8 7 6 5 4 3 2

CONTENTS

Chapter One

WHAT ARE REAL WORLD PARENTS?

I have a vivid memory of being a teenager and sitting at the dinner table with my family, rolling my eyes and pretending to gag behind my dad's back.

Why?

He was trying to do family devotions with us. But my three younger brothers and I just weren't buying it.

What Are Real World Parents?

Every four or five months my dad would hear some program on Christian radio about family devotions, and he'd come home with another new idea for making it work with our family. After all, that's what Christian families are supposed to do, right? But it just never worked in our house. It felt completely forced and unnatural.

Still, somehow all four of us Matlock boys ended up in ministry. My youngest brother, Jonathan, helped me start WisdomWorks Ministries, and now we both do pretty much the same kind of youth ministry and youth minister support through Youth Specialties. Our brother Josh is a senior pastor in Southern California, and our brother Jeremy is a missionary in Russia. And still to this day, whenever Dad tries to bring us together for "family devotions" during the holidays, we mock him a little. It's become a kind of tradition because it isn't genuine for who we are as a family.

Now, I'm not saying that having kids who serve in some area of ministry means you're a successful parent. The point I'm making is that all four of my dad's sons grew into men with a real passion and appreciation for God's Word—even though he couldn't get us to sit still and take the reading of the Word seriously during repeated failed attempts at family devotions.

Why? Because we knew *he* had a real passion and appreciation for God's Word. We saw Dad reading the Bible. We saw him struggle to apply it to his life. We saw both of our parents base their decisions on their understanding of what the Bible teaches.

Ultimately we were convinced of the worldview contained in the pages of Scripture because we saw our parents openly endorsing it, talking about it, learning from it, and living it out day after day, year after year. That was enough for us—despite the failed attempts at family devotions.

That's what this book is about. We're not interested in presenting more artificial techniques and methodology to "fix" our kids or do what Christian families are "supposed to do." Rather we want to help you discover how to live for God in a real way, right in front of your kids, so they can't help but catch the big picture that God and his Word mean the world to us and that living for Jesus really works in the Real World.

Don't get me wrong. Not all families are built to the same specifications. We each have our own family DNA. So if family devotions fit who you are, more power to you! Organized, structured, traditional family devotions are a great tool for some families. Now that my wife, Jade, and I have two kids of our own—our son Dax is in middle school, and our daughter Skye is 10—we've tried to have a family Bible hour around the table. It kind of worked off and on when the kids were younger, but we eventually realized it wasn't a good fit for the natural rhythm of our lives. It's not who we are right now. So instead we've found ways to talk about God's Word that are a better fit for us.

As we work together through the concepts in this book, one thing we'll discover is that Real World Parents are real in the sense that they do what best fits their families, and they genuinely adjust their own lives to fit into God's story.

Is God Happy with My Family?

In the church today, there's some really good teaching on parenting. My wife and I have benefited from writers, conference speakers, and pastors who've opened God's Word and helped us connect with what it means to raise up our children in the way they should go, how to provide godly discipline, and ideas for reinforcing good behavior. But again, that's not what this book is about.

And, honestly, over the years I've been frustrated with some teaching on parenting that's built around making parents feel guilty. These teachers, authors, books, and programs build parenting models based on our common fear that we're going to mess up our kids—or that we've *already* messed up our kids. That's an easy road that plays on our fears and our guilt over the areas in which we struggle as parents. Then they suggest that their programs or perspectives are our final hope to "get it right" or, worse, to do it the only way God wants it done.

That's not what this book is about, either. I promise not to use your parenting fears and anxieties against you. And we all have those feelings. I know I have them. If you could spend a little time with my family, you'd quickly see that we have issues, too. Those prone to critiquing parents would have no trouble criticizing my wife and me. So, no, I'm not interested in beating up other parents in order to somehow make them feel better or more motivated in their parenting.

In fact, I'd like to communicate exactly the opposite.

In our Real World Parent seminars, held around the United States, our teachers use a self-diagnostic tool to help attendees identify what they believe God thinks of their families.

It goes something like this:

What do you think God sees when he looks at your family? Do you think God grins or grimaces? (Place an X on the line.)

GOD GRINS ————————————— GOD GRIMACES

This can be a challenging question if you take it seriously. On one hand, those of us who've grown up in Christian churches understand the idea of God's grace. We understand that our relationship with God isn't based on our performance. God sacrificed his only Son—the Son whom God loves so deeply—to pay for our sins on a cross. And God did this long before we even knew we wanted that gift from God. Thus, we'd always check the box that says God's love is unconditional for those of us in Christ.

Still, we have trouble carrying the idea of God's grace into our parenting. We can talk ourselves into believing that failing our kids is an unforgivable sin, that God could never be pleased with us if we've been guilty of sloppy or harsh or inconsistent or selfish or fearful or overprotective or neglectful parenting.

We may wonder how God could ever look at our families and grin. And the problem is that, as parents, we sometimes forget that we're also children—that our God is our Father, and that God is more lovingly inclined to smile at us than we are to smile at our own kids. Our Father loves us, and he forgives our parenting shortcomings and our family failings.

I will say this more than once: *Nothing you read in this book will make God the Father love you and your family any more than he does right now, no matter what's going on with your family today.*

I made this statement at one of our Real World Parent seminars, and I noticed that one of the women began to cry. She came up to me later and explained how inferior she's felt as a mother in her local church. Her husband isn't a believer, her kids get into trouble, and she just felt like such a failure—like a second-class parent in a church where most of the other parents were both Christians, still married, and raising such "nice" children.

I tried to assure her that God's grace applies to us as parents, and that in Christ she is forgiven and fully accepted as a beloved daughter (and mom!). The idea that God loved her family right now—in its present condition—was a reality she wasn't living in. She felt she was "underperforming" as a parent and couldn't keep up. So she said the idea that she's forgiven, accepted, and loved as a parent gave her immense comfort.

Ernest Hemingway's short story called "The Capital of the World" begins with an anecdote about a man in Madrid who put an ad in the newspaper to contact his estranged son. The ad read, PACO, MEET ME AT HOTEL MONTANA NOON TUESDAY. ALL IS FORGIVEN. PAPA. The story then describes how at noon on Tuesday, 800 young men arrived at the hotel to make peace with their fathers.

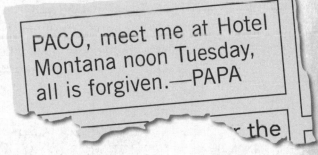

PACO, meet me at Hotel Montana noon Tuesday, all is forgiven.—PAPA

The joke was that there are lots of guys in Spain named Paco. But the other message is that wanting our dads' approval, specifically, is a universal human experience. Taking nothing away from the indispensable role of our mothers, we all long to have our fathers sign off on who we are and what we're doing.

It's what psychologists call "father hunger."

As Christians, followers of Jesus, we have that hunger even in our roles as parents, even if we've made mistakes along the way. Our Father has forgiven us. We live in God's grace. God approves of us in Christ. And, yes, God loves us.

I want to make it perfectly clear—again—that you'll find no directives in this book that will make God love you or your family even a little bit more than he already does. God's unconditional love for your family was established long ago. It is full. It cannot grow. Romans 8:1 declares, "Therefore, there is now no condemnation for those who are in Christ Jesus." And that includes Christian parents.

I hope you've heard that. But I also hope you aren't satisfied to leave your family where it is today. Because while I'm convinced that God will never love or accept you any more than he does right now, I'm also convinced that God loves you so much that he won't leave you where you are right now, either.

No matter how good or bad you believe your family is, God has plans for you that will unfold in the Real World. God will continue to move your family along in the journey he has in store for you. Which is why this book is designed to help Real World Parents understand that journey—or story—and communicate it to our kids.

"How Will This Book Fix My Kids?"

As long as we're talking about things this book isn't, I should mention again that in the following pages you won't find any tips or tricks or techniques to fix your children's bad behavior. (We'd probably sell more copies if that's what we were promising, but we're not.)

In my experience, books full of tips, techniques, and tricks succeed at making readers feel good for a while. They make us feel hopeful. They make us feel as though we're *doing something* about the problem. But they often fail in the long run because we just can't keep it up. We can't change the personalities of our families to fit the models of the new programs on an ongoing basis.

When my kids came along, though, and I started making my way through all the different kinds of Christian parenting books, I noticed that a lot of them focused on helping me raise well-behaved, well-mannered kids. And while that's an important element, there wasn't much focus on raising kids to have hearts that seek after Christ. Of course we can't force that kind of spiritual openness and connectedness with God onto our kids—but in our Real World homes, we can create environments that promote such growth.

In a sense we become gardeners tending the spiritual development of our kids. God places the spark of life in the seed. We can't control that or how the plant eventually matures. But we can make sure the soil is rich, the ground is generously watered, the weeds are kept at bay, and the opportunity for sunlight is freely available. We can raise our children in environments where having a heart for God is the norm and not the exception.

What we don't want to generate are well-behaved kids who mindlessly follow our directions without ever willfully owning the faith in Jesus that they see in us. In the long run, the goal of parenting isn't for our kids to be known for how well-behaved they are, but for how well they know and respond to God.

Part of our challenge is to communicate to our kids a worldview that supports right actions. It's true that we (and they) will be held accountable for our behavior based on God's instructions to us. But whether or not we obey those instructions has a lot to do with whether or not we really believe God's story—a biblical worldview—and whether or not we walk in God's power.

In that way, our children's behavior is kind of like the tip of an iceberg. From countless illustrations we all know that the part of the iceberg that rises above the waterline is just a fraction of its total size. As such, you could conceivably make all kinds of alterations to the exposed part of the iceberg—in other words, the outward stuff (behaviors)—without significantly altering the iceberg itself.

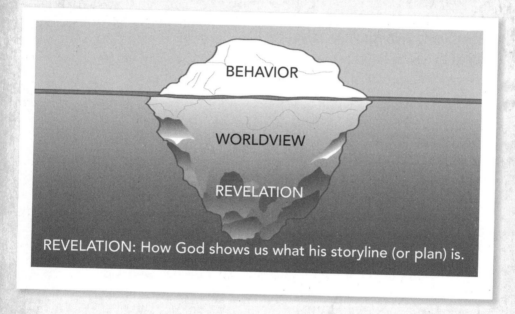

BEHAVIOR

WORLDVIEW

REVELATION

REVELATION: How God shows us what his storyline (or plan) is.

What we've got to get at—in our own lives and in the lives of our kids—is the 80 percent of the berg that's under the waterline. In our illustration that represents one's worldview. We believe our behavior is ultimately driven by our understanding of the way the world works, of what we believe to be true and false about the universe, of our perception of reality.

And *that's* what we want to focus on as Real World Parents. How can we communicate God's worldview to our kids?

What story are we telling them about the universe, both intentionally and—more importantly—in the way we live with and for God over time?

Before you move on to the next chapter, ask yourself these questions:

1. When you imagine God looking at your family, what do you think God sees? What do you believe God's desire for your family is?

2. When you look at the world your children are living in, do you believe it's better or worse compared to when you were growing up? Why?

3. Which matters more to you—that your children demonstrate good behavior, or that your children understand and believe in a biblical worldview? Why?

4. In your own life, what has mattered more in the long run—your behavior on any given day or your foundational beliefs about God and the world?

Chapter Two

WHAT'S THE REAL STORY?

Star Wars is one of my favorite movies of all time, but I especially loved it when I was a kid. I just couldn't get enough of that story. And like all kids, I identified with the characters, putting myself in their shoes. While I was watching it recently (for the 39th time), I *was* Luke Skywalker. And then I *was* Han Solo. I lived in that story for those 90 or so minutes.

Imagine, though, that I'm watching Star Wars and Bo and Luke Duke suddenly show up in The General Lee, racing around the Death Star while sounding Dixie on the horn. I would be furious!

What's the Real Story?

Now, I love *The Dukes of Hazzard*, but those two stories don't fit together. It would bother me to see them forced on top of each other, sharing the same space and time. Boss Hogg should never have a lightsaber. Period.

It's a silly illustration to make a serious point. Some of us try to live in two stories at the same time—and we're telling both stories to our kids. On one hand we want them to understand and live in God's story of the universe. And on the other hand, we hold to what we visualize as a "real world" story for the other half of our lives. Sometimes these stories seem to match up, and sometimes they seem as many worlds apart as Darth Vader and Daisy Duke.

From Little-R to Big-R

We don't always mean to, but we all walk around inside two distinct realities. I call the first our "little-R" reality—our personal perspectives on how the world works. The second is God's version—the "big-R" reality—which is absolutely true and complete in every aspect. God's view of reality is perfect.

Why do we give God credit for having the ultimate view of reality? It's too easy to say, "Because he's God," but that's the gist of it. His being God means several key and important things to Christians. And these attributes convince us that God's version of reality must be the only right one.

First, God is *eternal*. God has always existed and will always exist. Psalm 90 puts it in poetry: "Before the mountains were born or you brought forth the earth and the world, from everlasting to everlasting you are God" (verse 2). God is the only One who's always been here, so God is the only one who knows the whole story from start to finish.

Second, God knows everything. God is *omniscient*. Psalm 147: "Great is our Lord and mighty in power; his understanding has no limit" (verse 5).

Next, God has all the power to do exactly what he wants at all times. God creates reality as he pleases. We call that *omnipotence*. Nothing falls out of the realm of what's possible for God: "I am the Lord, the God of all mankind. Is anything too hard for me?" (Jeremiah 32:37)

And if all that weren't enough, God is the *Creator*. God created us and the Real World we live in. God designed and built our reality from the ground up and placed us in the middle of it. So we take it as a given that God's view of reality trumps all, that God's perspective is always the correct perspective. But still, it's not the reality we live in from day to day.

Why not? For one thing, God hasn't disclosed every detail of the big-R reality. God has kept some of it hidden. And some truth about God's universe would likely be difficult for us to understand and process.

The other reason we're missing parts of God's perspective of the universe—God's reality—is that we haven't fully absorbed what God has revealed to us through creation, through his Word, and through our experience with him.

Still, that's our goal as people and as parents—to get our little-R realities to fit inside God's big-R reality, to fit both our understanding of the universe and our response to it inside what we know about God's understanding of the universe.

Practically speaking, why wouldn't we want to live that way? Why would we want to spend our lives desperately trying to shoehorn our false views of reality into God's true story of the world?

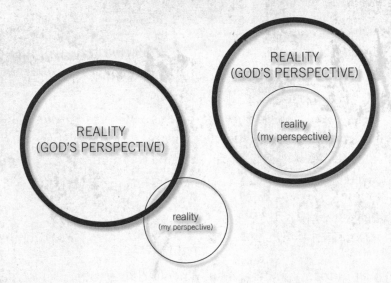

No, the more we're capable of living in God's reality from God's perspective, the healthier our families will be.

And that means we must be very careful about what stories we listen to and believe. Our little-R reality is a very soft thing. From the big truths of life to our perceptions of the everyday facts all around us, our perspectives are shaped by a lot of different influences. And from all those inputs, we build the story our families live in.

I use the word *story* intentionally. We use our understanding of the world to define our settings, to turn the people in our lives into characters, and to make sense of the plot unfolding around us from day to day. And then we tell our kids that story—that version of reality—and they begin to respond to it.

Parenting According to the Wrong Story

Sometimes Christian parents are absolutely convinced about the big truths of God's story of the universe—creation, the virgin birth, God's love for the world, Jesus' death on the cross for our sins—but still arrive at some wrong conclusions about the way that story is playing out in the world right now.

And sometimes the church and those who market messages to the church don't help parents come up with the right story, either.

Here's another diagnostic question we use in our Real World Parent seminars to help people evaluate what story they're living in by placing an X on the continuum somewhere between:

It's a good time _____ It's a bad time
 to be a parent.   to be a parent.

Or putting it another way: When it comes to teen involvement in drinking, smoking, and sexual choices, do you believe things have gotten better or worse in the last 20 years?

Our answers to these questions are shaped by the stories we hear in the secular media and even from Christian writers and speakers. And those of us who live in a church subculture have even more people telling us stories than those who don't. That's because we're listening both inside and outside the walls.

Frankly, sometimes the messages that come from *inside* the walls are distorted or just flat-out untrue. Why? For one thing, a certain segment of Christian storytelling is heavily dependent on selling books, filling chairs, and raising money. That segment is driven to tell stories that sell, that motivate a specific kind of action. And it's easy to slant the story in ways that don't line up with reality.

In other words, sometimes it's helpful to those trying to sell a story if it demonstrates that everything is continually getting worse, because that motivates well-intentioned people to pay attention or write checks. The fallout for parents, though, can be a lot of fear and misperception about the world their kids are living in—and we end up telling them the wrong story.

So...are things getting continually worse? Let's look at some recent statistics. (You can find our sources for these stats listed at the end of the chapter.)

One qualifier before we jump in: *By no means am I suggesting that any of these numbers tell a good story about the state of the world today.* In fact, you'll soon see that they confirm the teaching of God's Word that says we humans are a fallen species (Romans 3:22-24). However, these numbers also challenge the idea that everything is continually getting worse in their kids' world.

MARRIAGE

Most of us would probably say that the state of marriage in America is a subject for concern. While I'm not saying we *shouldn't* be concerned, the situation may not be as bad as some might suggest.

Back in 1960, there were about 9.2 divorces a year for every 1,000 women aged 15 and older. By 1970, that number had started to climb, and by 1980 it reached a high point of 22.6 divorces per year per 1,000 married women.

MARRIAGE GRAPH[1]   **Divorces per 1,000 married women, age 15+**

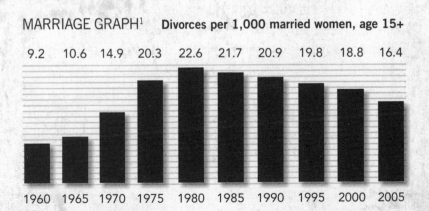

9.2	10.6	14.9	20.3	22.6	21.7	20.9	19.8	18.8	16.4
1960	1965	1970	1975	1980	1985	1990	1995	2000	2005

1. David Popenoe, "The Future of Marriage in America," *The State of Our Unions: The Social Health of Marriage in America 2007,* http://marriage.rutgers.edu/Publications/SOOU/TEXTSOOU2007.htm

What was going on during this time period to create such a rapid increase in divorce? For one thing, there was the introduction of the no-fault divorce. People could get out of their marriages without any justifiable claim against their spouses. And by 1975, many of the most populated states in the Union had adopted the no-fault divorce. More and more people were getting divorced for no good reason. We saw that number peak in 1980.

But take a look at what's happened since then: Those numbers have slowly and steadily declined. This is a really different picture from what many of us have come to believe about the state of divorce—it's a different story than the one we've been told.

In fact, when we look at the numbers in 2005, they're almost back to where they were in 1970. And we have reason to believe those numbers will taper off just a little bit more before reaching a stabilizing point.

Americans haven't given up on the hope of marriage. In fact, in an international survey, only 10 percent of Americans agreed that "marriage is an outdated institution."[2] It's true that people are waiting longer to get married, and that the number of cohabiting couples has increased somewhat. These trends need to be watched. But the declining rate of divorce indicates that things may not be getting "worse."

So why is our collective perception so radically different? It might have to do with the fact that it's become much less shameful in our society to live together and to talk about it openly. In fact, until the 1970s, it was illegal to cohabitate in many states. The U.S. Census didn't even track unmarried couples living together until after 1996. So we're more aware of cohabitation today, but the number of people practicing it is actually pretty small.

---

2. Ibid., see "The European Direction."

In addition, 85 percent of Americans expect to marry sometime in their lives. Also, 82 percent of female high school seniors and 70 percent of males say that "having a good marriage and family life" is "extremely important" to them.

Marriage isn't on its way out, after all. In fact, it seems really healthy and vibrant.

SEXUAL CHOICES

Traditional marriage might be doing okay—even in spite of the recent pushes for the legalization of gay marriage.

But we know that too many teens *are* having sex, right? Well, yes, too many teens are having sex. But are the numbers getting worse? These answers may surprise you, as well.

Indirectly related, first of all, was the 2005 birth rate for 15- to 17-year-old girls—the lowest in U.S. history. Since birth control accounts for just a fraction of that decrease, this was a major milestone for our country in terms of teens making better choices. And while new studies are reporting a slight birth-rate increase in 2006, it hasn't erased the overall progress that's been made in previous years.[3]

Bottom line: We're finding that more teenagers are delaying sexual intercourse. The number of high school students who report having sexual intercourse at least once dropped from 54 percent in 1991 to 46 percent in 2001. That percentage has remained steady in this decade.[4]

3. Kristin Anderson Moore, "Teen Births: Examining the Recent Increase," *Trends Research Brief* (March 2009), http://www.childtrends.org/Files//Child_Trends_2009_03_13_FS_TeenBirthRate.pdf.

4. Elizabeth Terry-Humen, Jennifer Manlove, and Sarah Cottingham, "Trends and Recent Estimates: Sexual Activity Among U.S. Teens," *Trends Research Brief* (June 2006). http://www.childtrends.org/Files//Child_Trends-2006_06_01_RB_SexualActivity.pdf.

Tucked inside *that* number is an 11-point drop in sexual intercourse among all 11th graders, a 14-point drop among all black students, and a 10-point drop among all male students.

The number of high school seniors who report having sexual intercourse at least once has never dropped below 60 percent, but more kids—and, notably, more boys—are waiting longer. The trend is edging in a positive direction.

Is that a different story than the one you've been hearing? Okay, but what about oral sex? Aren't kids just doing that instead of having traditional sex? "That's what I've heard," you might say. But the numbers don't completely support that notion, either.

Studies looking at oral sex among teenagers do show a surprisingly high percentage of youth participating in oral sex, but it's not replacing vaginal intercourse. About 16 percent of 15- to-17-year-olds in 2002 have had oral sex—but haven't yet had sexual intercourse.[5] It's generally something that comes after the fact. Very few kids are living the "technical virgin" life. And that runs contrary to the stories we've heard, as well.

How does that happen? How do we get such a wrong impression? Well, a lot of people stand to profit from the stories that say everything's on the decline. And sometimes these shaky stories just build momentum and start rolling downhill. Plus, several events happened in a very short timeframe, thereby giving the impression that oral sex was rampant.

First, we came out of the Bill Clinton-Monica Lewinski scandal, so it was in the national psyche. Next, a group of teenagers in Ohio got busted in a sex-party scandal, and it made national news. Then the author of a popular book introduced us to the

5. Ibid., see p. 3 of study.

idea of "rainbow parties"—kids getting together and engaging in oral sex. Even at the time, many believed it was a questionable story and suggested the book actually promoted the practice instead of warning us about it. But the story had already been told, and it stuck.

Picking up on that book and the Ohio scandal and the national sensitivity to all of it, Oprah Winfrey started doing shows on oral sex. Then Dr. Phil followed suit on his own television show. And pretty soon we had this idea, this story, in our psyche that teenagers were having oral sex like crazy when the national numbers didn't support it.

But even so, the story still shapes us and influences us more than the reality does. This and other marginal stories get built into our little-R reality and influence the way we parent our kids.

Here's another variation from the story: Despite what many of us may assume, most teen girls who get pregnant do *not* do so with teen guys. Rather, a full 65 percent are impregnated by men over the age of 20. That means the biggest part of this problem isn't about teens having sex with each other and getting pregnant; it's about adult men, age 20 and older, having sex with teen girls.[6]

In fact, girls under the age of 15 who become pregnant are six times more likely to have paired up with a man older than 20 than with a peer.

Is that a shocking and bad number? Yes, of course it is. But understanding the reality instead of the false story can help us better prepare and parent our kids. It tells us that if we can teach our daughters to deflect the attention of grown

---

6. "Teens and Older Partners," Michael Males, Resource Center for Adolescent Pregnancy Prevention, May-June 2004, http://www.etr.org/recapp/index.cfm?fuseaction=pages.currentresearchdetail&PageID=393&PageTypeID=18

men, the rates of teenage sexual intercourse and pregnancy will fall even further.

Please don't get me wrong. I'm not trying to tell you that things are better in your specific area than they really are. Because if kids in your home are having sex, then that's a big deal—regardless of what the rest of the country is experiencing. And it should be. I'm not suggesting we should remove all limits on our kids because they're never going to have sex. That's not even the point.

But I do believe this: If we're parenting out of fear based on incomplete stories, then we're less likely to make the right decisions. We need to be open to reevaluating our assumptions and rethinking the stories we've believed for so long.

For instance, when researchers studied high school seniors over the last 20 years, 60 percent said they'd engaged in a sexual relationship before going on to college or into the work force. That number has remained steady for two decades.

So, no, things aren't necessarily getting *better*, but they aren't necessarily getting *worse*, either. Should we be satisfied with those numbers? No! And especially not if they're happening around us. But let's not inflate them and raise the alarm in order to motivate action beyond what's needed. Let's tell each other the truth and respond in ways that are appropriate.

More story adjusters:

SUICIDE

Completed adolescent suicides dropped nearly 30 percent from 1995 to 2003—even as the means of completed suicide became more violent.

The stories were getting more intense. The ways in which teens were ending their lives were becoming much more theatrical and dramatic. And, understandably, those kinds of horrible anecdotes stick with people. Therefore the impression many are left with is that the numbers are getting worse. But teen suicides have actually been dropping significantly.

Having said that, in 2004, the number of teen suicides rose a little bit—just enough to cause some concern that the trend might be reversing. But the uptick was minor; and based on the numbers now coming in from 2005, it looks as though that was just a blip on the radar, not a continuing projection. But we'll know more as numbers for 2006 and subsequent years are released.[7]

ADOLESCENT CRIME

When it comes to adolescent crime, there's a huge gap between the crime statistics and what the media reports is taking place in the world around us.

Juvenile felonies and incidents of gang violence peaked in 1993 and have fallen ever since. In Los Angeles alone, murder rates among black, Latino, and Asian youths fell 85 percent from 1993 to 1999.[8] That's dramatic.

In 1990, one black youth was arrested for murder every 80 hours in Los Angeles. By 2000, that number had declined to one arrest a month. That huge shift is a trend we see not just in L.A., but in other cities around the country, as well. Nationwide, adolescent violent crime dropped from 52 incidents per 1,000 kids in 1993 to 14 per 1,000 in 2005.

---

7. Centers for Disease Control and Prevention, "Suicide Trends Among Youths and Young Adults Aged 10-24 Years—United States, 1990–2004," *Morbidity and Mortality Weekly Report* 56 (35), September 7, 2007, http://www.cdc.gov/mmwr/preview/mmwrhtml/mm5635a2.htm.

8. "Get a Clue on Youth Violence," Mike Males, *Los Angeles Times*, April 25, 1999, http://articles.latimes.com/1999/apr/25/local/me-30847

As with suicide, though, we see a slight uptick beginning in 2005. For the first time in a decade, violent crimes against 15-to-17-year-olds and violent crimes committed by juveniles were up. There was a further small increase in 2006, but we don't know for sure if this is the beginning of a new trend.

One thing we *do* know for sure—even if it's a very different story than the one we're used to hearing—is that whites over the age of 30 perpetrate far more violent crimes across the nation than juveniles of all colors put together. Let me say it again just because it rings so false in our ears based on the stories we're usually told: *All the violent crimes committed by all the adolescents of every race are fewer in number than the violent crimes committed by white people over the age of 30.*

DRUG ABUSE

In 1980, 40 percent of American high school seniors misused drugs. That number has been up and down ever since, following a lot of different societal trends—dropping to nearly 15 percent in the early '90s and then back up to 26 percent in the early 2000s. The most recent statistics from 2008 show the rate of rate of drug abuse among high school seniors at around 22 percent.[9]

Nearly one-fourth of kids taking drugs is a terrible number. We wish it were zero. Still, some reading these words would've been convinced that drug use got bad in the '60s and '70s and has been getting steadily worse ever since. That's not the accurate story.

TOBACCO USE

Between 1995 and 2008, the number of middle and high school students who smoked daily reduced by half. That's significant.

---

9. Federal Interagency Forum on Child and Family Statistics, *America's Children: Key National Indicators of Well-Being*, 2009, http://www.childstats.gov/americaschildren/beh3.asp.

What does it tell us? Anti-smoking education is actually working, and the laws governing these things are working as well.[10]

BINGE DRINKING

Another place where we see the numbers getting better is in the area of binge drinking, which was defined in the study we researched as downing five or more adult beverages in a row. In 1980, more than 40 percent of high school seniors reported binge drinking in the two weeks prior to the survey. In 2008, the percentage stood at 25 percent. That's an enormous 15 percent drop.[11]

Many of us will have to change our stories in response to those numbers. Apparently, contemporary adolescents tend to make better choices about alcohol than their parents did at the same age. In fact, they tend to make better choices than many of their parents make today.

For example, twice as many 35-to-54-year-olds binge drink than do teenagers and college students combined. Think about that one for a moment. Look at that age window again.

Drinking among minors peaked in the 1980s, and then it declined.[12] But the teenagers who were binge drinking in the '80s are still doing it as adults! They've continued a lot of that behavior. It's likely that some of us were teenagers, or close to it, back in the '80s when a lot of these numbers were at their peak. Therefore, we must avoid the temptation to believe that things have steadily gotten worse since we were in high school.

10. Federal Interagency Forum on Child and Family Statistics, *America's Children: Key National Indicators of Well-Being*, 2009, http://www.childstats.gov/americaschildren/beh1.asp.

11. Federal Interagency Forum on Child and Family Statistics, *America's Children: Key National Indicators of Well-Being*, 2009, http://www.childstats.gov/americaschildren/beh2.asp.

12. Federal Interagency Forum on Child and Family Statistics, *America's Children: Key National Indicators of Well-Being*, 2009, http://www.childstats.gov/americaschildren/beh2.asp.

So What?

You might be wondering about the point of all these statistics. After all, even if things are getting better, many of the numbers are still awful. It's still scary to think about our kids living out there in and around those numbers. The world isn't a safe place.

That's all true, but I want us to understand that getting the story right *really* matters. It changes how we relate to our kids. It changes how we parent. And it keeps us from being easily manipulated by our increasingly story-driven, media-saturated society.

Over the last decade or two, the information game has completely changed. New to our mostly middle-aged generation is the onslaught of 24-hours-a-day, seven-days-a-week cable news stations, as well as news Web sites and moment-by-moment Twitter news services. We were born into a world in which news came in a morning paper and mostly focused on stories about local and regional events. That world is gone.

Today's news teams are striving to feed that information monster with a new batch of stories every hour. To keep the money rolling in, they must keep eyeballs stuck to their stories all day long, whether those eyes watch computer screens, TVs, or iPhones. So they're compelled to tell the most salacious, most terrifying, most sensational, most heated stories they can possibly generate.

The fallout is that we're left focusing on the wrong things, walking around with vast misconceptions, thanks to our little-R realities, and lacking the big-R reality. For instance, did you know that the number of child abductions is down in our country? Yet in a recent survey, most parents believed kidnappings are on the rise. Why? For one thing, we live in the era of the

What's the Real Story?

Amber Alert, which notifies us on a large scale (through various media outlets) every time a child is believed abducted.

The hope is to create tighter nets to rescue those kids and get them home. It's a fantastic, well-intentioned idea. However, we're now aware of practically all abductions soon after they occur, whereas prior to the creation of the Amber Alert system in 1996, we may not have been aware of them at all. Slowly we begin to tell ourselves a different story: More kids are being abducted.

This story distorts our perception of the reality we live in. We don't tend to focus on the fact that most abductions are perpetrated by people the children know and that even those numbers are declining. Instead we continue to believe that "stranger danger" is more dangerous than ever.

If we believe the world is a scary, awful place that's getting more and more evil every day, it'll affect the way we raise our kids. So we have to ask ourselves important questions about who we're listening to, and what we're believing. We have to ask ourselves, *Does this story add up?*

Christianity Today ran an article in 2007 called "Evangelicals Behaving Badly with Statistics." It basically slapped the hands of several well-known Christian leaders for inappropriately using statistics to serve their own ministry purposes and goals by striking fear into the hearts of pastors and parents across the country.

The statistics they presented weren't accurate, which means their stories were false. In some cases, the storytellers couldn't find any sources for the stats they quoted. When pressed, a few said their conclusions were based on their hunches, their feelings about what was probably going on in the world out there.

That's a problem. We tend to listen to people of influence in our lives, but when those people give us inaccurate information, we suffer because the information presented causes us to change our stories, change the way we raise our kids. It's so important to make sure we're not parenting based on a collection of false assumptions.

Instead, we need to live in a story that exists within God's big-R reality, a story that's completely true, the Real World story that our families are creating as we walk together along the path on which God has placed us. In the next chapter, we'll look at a very different study that reaches some positive and encouraging conclusions about the stories Christian parents tell (and show!) their children.

Sources

My point is that there are concerns we need to address and be mindful of as parents—but overall these problems aren't necessarily getting worse. Many of the sources I've cited include Web sites that provide updates to data and trends as they become available, if you're interested in learning more.

America's Children: Key National Indicators of Well-Being, 2009
(http://www.childstats.gov/AMERICASCHILDREN/index.asp)

Dishonest Youth Videos by Mike Males
(http://home.earthlink.net/~mmales/yt-mef.htm)

Enabling Adult Immaturity by Mike Males
(http://home.earthlink.net/~mmales/yt-binge.htm)

Gutless about Gut Issues by Mike Males
(http://home.earthlink.net/~mmales/yt-obese.htm)

What's the Real Story?

Kids and Guns: How Politicians, Experts, and the Press Fabricate Fear of Youth by Mike Males (http://home.earthlink.net/~mmales/contents.htm)

Nearly 3 in 10 Young Teens 'Sexually Active' by Ana Maria Arumi (http://www.msnbc.msn.com/id/6839072/)

Pubertal Transitions in Health by George C. Patton and Russell Viner (http://www.thelancet.com/journals/lancet/article/PIIS0140-6736(07)60366-3/abstract); free registration needed to access full text

Report: Teen Birth Rate Hits Record Low (http://www.usatoday.com/news/health/2007-07-16-3524503849_x.htm)

Report of the APA Task Force on the Sexualization of Girls (http://www.apa.org/pi/wpo/sexualization.html)

Sexual Behavior and Selected Health Measures: Men and Women 15-44 Years of Age, United States, 2002 (http://www.cdc.gov)

The State of Our Unions: The Social Health of Marriage in America 2007 by David Popenoe (http://marriage.rutgers.edu/Publications/SOOU/TEXTSOOU2007.htm)

Suicide Trends Among Youths and Young Adults Aged 10-24 Years—United States, 1990–2004 (http://www.cdc.gov/mmwr/preview/mmwrhtml/mm5635a2.htm)

Trends and Recent Estimates: Sexual Activity Among U.S. Teens by Elizabeth Terry-Humen, Jennifer Manlove, and Sarah Cottingham (www.childtrends.org/files/SexualActivityRB.pdf)

U.S. Crime 1970–2000 (http://home.earthlink.net/~mmales/uscrime.txt)

U.S. Teenage Pregnancy Statistics: Overall Trends, Trends by Race and Ethnicity and State-by-State Information by the Guttmacher Institute (http://www.guttmacher.org/pubs/teen_preg_stats.html)

Before you move on to the next chapter, ask yourself these questions:

1. Why is God most qualified to define what truth is? Why is God's story of reality the most reliable one?

2. Would you say this is a good or bad time to be a parent? On what information have you been basing your conclusion? What makes any time a good or bad time to parent a child?

3. Do you believe things have gotten better or worse in the last 20 years—or in the time since you were in high school?

4. Does your perception of reality lead to parenting from within God's story or a false idea about the state of the world?

Chapter Three

WHAT STORY ARE WE TELLING?

Obviously, none of us want to build our families' stories on a set of statistics. If you survived all those numbers in the last chapter, I applaud you. As American statesman Henry Clay once said, "Statistics are no substitute for judgment."

And Aaron Levenstein, professor emeritus at Baruch College, said, "Statistics are like a bikini. What they reveal is suggestive, but what they conceal is vital." (I don't know what that means, but I thought it sounded funny.)

What Story Are We Telling?

I hope you have the stomach for the results of one more study, though, because I believe you'll find it encouraging. It's really more about using some seriously collected statistics (that we're not going to look at) to come to some extremely helpful bottom-line conclusions for parents.

Researchers Christian Smith and Lisa Pearce were given a sizable grant to study the faith beliefs of adolescents, and the results of their work are fascinating. It's called the National Study of Youth and Religion (youthandreligion.org), and the findings are based on thousands of interviews with teenagers across the nation.

Now, these results aren't specifically targeted toward Christians. Smith and Pearce interviewed teens of many religious (or non-religious) beliefs. But the results we'll examine here use their measurements of what they call "spiritually healthy" kids, and I believe it's safe to apply them in the broadest terms to the story we walk in with our own kids. (We'll talk about how this fits into a biblical worldview later in the chapter.)

So according to this study, what does it take for kids to become spiritually healthy? Three things:

1. STRONG AND CLEAR EXPECTATIONS WITH BOUNDARIES, DEMANDS, AND ACCOUNTABILITY

Kids thrive within clearly drawn lines, but we're not talking about simply ruling with an iron fist and laying down the law. The study shows that kids benefit most from understanding why those lines are there and what greater purpose they serve. Effective parents are proactive about educating their children about the reasons for these parameters and then holding them accountable to stay within them.

2. EMOTIONAL WARMTH AND CLOSENESS

This means helping kids experience the truth that they are loved. That involves more than just telling them we love them and proving our love by providing for their basic physical needs. It's showing our love with touch, smiles, time together, gentle words, and whatever else it takes to help them feel closely connected to other people.

3. COGNITIVE AUTONOMY

This means creating space to work things out and making room for children to reach positions that aren't exactly the same as their parents' in every instance. In other words, kids are allowed to push back with ideas of their own without fear of being shut down—and do so within the safety and acceptance of their parents' nurturing care. The study found this approach helps kids develop a vibrant faith of their own.

It's easy to read through these three big areas of parenting and kind of nod and move on. But if you see yourself in the business of raising spiritually healthy Christian kids, it might be worth spending a little time applying these ideas to your specific situation at home.

Got a piece of paper and a few minutes? Try this.

1. Write down three of the most important boundaries you've set for your kids. Big ones. Really important ones. Now read these questions and rate yourself on a scale from 1 to 10, with 10 being highest:

    How clearly do my kids understand what the boundary or rule is? How clearly do they understand why it exists? How consistent have I been in enforcing the boundary?

2. Rate yourself on these measures of warmth and closeness:

   How likely is it that my kids know I love them right now? How likely is it that they feel loved by me right now? How likely is it that they'd feel comfortable moving closer to me when they feel the need for connection?

3. Rate yourself on these measures of cognitive autonomy:

   How open am I to hearing my kids express ideas or beliefs that are different from my own? How likely are they to share with me their doubts or hard questions about the beliefs I've taught them? To what extent have they claimed ownership of (verbally or with acts of commitment to) the beliefs they've been raised with?

These are hard questions and, yes, I do remember my earlier promise to not beat up on parents in this book. So I hope that asking yourself these questions doesn't make you feel beaten up. For me, they're just motivational tools I can use to look for opportunities to give my kids what they need to grow healthier spiritually.

Storytelling Starts at Home

But how can we as Christian parents make sure our kids are coming to understand and live in God's story for the universe and God's story for their lives?

Too often we believe it's the church's job to tell our kids God's story and to make sure they know God, Scripture, and their responsibility to follow both. Not only is that approach flat-out wrong, but Christian Smith's research also indicates that it doesn't work. After talking to thousands of teenagers, he's found that the ones who really take ownership of their parents' understanding of the story of God are the ones who've heard and seen that story modeled at home.

As Smith puts it in his study, a parent is "the most important pastor a teenager will ever have." God calls us as moms and dads to shepherd our kids, to guide them into the right understanding of God's big-R reality, God's story of the universe.

The only way we parents can effectively accomplish this is by living in that story ourselves—day after day after day—so that talking about God and God's Word becomes as natural a part of our family life as talking about school and sports and what's for dinner. If our kids don't hear and observe that God's revelation through his Word is important to us, then why would it ever be important to them?

Deuteronomy 6:4-9 contains a prayer the Jewish faithful called the *shema*. They recited it daily, both when they woke up and before they went to bed. And it may be the clearest expression of being a Real World parent:

> "Hear, O Israel: The LORD our God, the LORD is one. Love the LORD your God with all your heart and with all your soul and with all your strength. These commandments that I give you today are to be upon your hearts. Impress them on your children. Talk about them when you sit at home and when you walk along the road, when you lie down and when you get up. Tie them as symbols on your hands and bind them on your foreheads. Write them on the doorframes of your houses and on your gates."

Later we'll marry these ideas to a New Testament understanding of Jesus. But this passage effectively captures one of the biggest ideas about God's story—an essential part of God's perspective, his big-R reality: *The Lord is one.*

Unlike so many other religious people at the time this prayer was written, Israelites followed one God and only one God. More, they discounted all the other gods as worthless hunks of wood, stone, and metal. Understanding God's story begins with understanding that he's the only God.

Next, this passage shows us how this one God intends for us to respond to the elemental truth that he is God: *Love him.* That's the story God wants us to walk in—loving him with everything we have and working to incorporate every aspect of his revelation into the very fibers of our hearts.

Then this passage reveals that part of our story is about telling God's story to our children. If we're parents, God's will is for us to tell his story to our kids—and to keep telling it over and over and over again as a part of our everyday waking-up, brushing-teeth, eating-breakfast, going-to-bed lives.

Real World parenting is about including God in our real world to the point that our kids cannot miss it. If they're convinced that *we're* convinced about God, it will become much easier for them to respond to God in a genuine way as well.

Okay, I know from experience that some of you are squirming at that idea. You're wishing that this really were a book full of tips and tricks for changing your kids' behavior. But instead, it's a book about changing our own lives from the inside out and showing our kids how doing so has changed everything.

Some will wonder how this manifesto fits with my childhood story about my family not doing devotions together because they weren't genuine to who we are as a family. But from my point of view, that particular vehicle for talking about God's story didn't fit the real world of our family's everyday life.

However, if talking about God *never* fits into the real world of our everyday lives, then we're not living in the real world of God's story.

Building on Revelation

What we're talking about here is clearly a long-term strategy. It's not about attacking the tip of that iceberg, about fixing the bad behaviors we see today. It's about building God's revelation into what's below the waterline. It's about communicating God's Word—as well as who God has revealed himself to be through creation—to our kids through everything we do, through every bit of who we are as parents.

We take what God has revealed, and we make interpretations. We try to understand it. We try to figure out how it integrates with our lives. And that gives us a worldview—specific values and beliefs about the world we live in. That value system and those beliefs, then, ultimately create and define our behavior.

Now, as adults we can think abstractly about concepts such as *revelation* and *worldview*. But how do our kids pick this up? How do we transfer these ideas to our kids' understanding, especially those of you with really young kids? We can't exactly show children this model and say, "What we want to do is shore up the concept of revelation. Son, I'm going to share with you this worldview change that you need to make in your life. And I hope it eventually corrects your errant behavior."

No, we need a plan. And as it turns out, that plan isn't all that different from how we adults incorporate God's revela-

What Story Are We Telling?

tion into our own lives. Here it is: *We talk about it. A lot. We tell stories about it. We fit our stories into God's one big story. And then we talk about it some more.*

Story is ultimately what happens below the waterline. Scripture is basically a series of stories—God's story of creation, redemption, God's interaction with mankind, and the hope God gives us for the future. It's a big, amazing story full of arresting smaller stories.

Yet we sometimes destroy it by chopping it up into a bunch of pieces that seem completely unrelated. Then we forget how they're supposed to fit back together again, and we get frustrated because we can't hold all of these pieces in our minds simultaneously. But when God's Word is viewed as one continuous story, it shapes our lives much more naturally. And when we base our story on fitting into God's story, we naturally weave the two stories inseparably together—exactly as we hope our children will do.

For instance, if I truly believe that Jesus is the way and the truth and the life, that's going to change the way I see the world. My belief tells me that other people need to know this great news, too—that Jesus Christ died for their sins, that Jesus can set them free from the bondage of sin.

I don't remember hearing the words, but I do remember seeing the lesson preached loudly in my dad's life once. Dad enjoyed Corvettes, but he could never bring himself to buy something so conspicuous. Still, after he did some work for a car dealership, he allowed himself to accept a Corvette as part of a barter agreement. He loved that car!

Then one day my brother Josh ran into it. Actually, he backed into it and punched a hole in the side of the car. Dad's response to Josh convinced me that he was living for God's storyline and not for the world's. Yes, he was upset with Josh for being careless, but he didn't become overly harsh or punish Josh for the accident. And as it turned out, he couldn't afford to get the car fixed right away—partly because of some financial commitments he'd made to some missions work. So Dad drove that Corvette with a big hole in the side, seemingly without a second thought.

Dad's reaction made it clear to all of us that he didn't define himself by his car. He defined himself by his God.

Indeed, every day we're telling our kids one story or another—and often without speaking a word. In the next chapter, we'll take a closer look at the storyline that's directly competing with the one we hope to tell our kids about living in the Real World of God's kingdom.

Before you move on to the next chapter, ask yourself these questions:

1. Do you believe you are the most important pastor your children will ever have? Why or why not?

2. Is the story you're telling your family (in the way you live your life with them) the same story of life and the world you hope they'll live in? Is it the same as God's story from the Bible?

3. How much of your day-to-day conversation with and around your family has to do with what God has revealed about truth, the universe, and himself?

Chapter Four

BROKEN STRATEGIES FOR COMPETING WITH THE WORLD'S STORY

Parenting would be a whole lot easier if all we had to do was tell God's story to our kids. If we existed in some cosmic diner where God's storyline was the only one on the menu, we and our kids would have no other choice but to embrace it in our thoughts, words, and actions every moment of every day.

Of course, there's another option on the menu. It's lethal, but sometimes it looks strangely appetizing to us. And because of sin, our kids come with a built-in taste for that second blue plate special, as well. It's called the world's storyline, and it's offered in direct competition to God's revealed perspective on how the universe really works.

Life has two competing storylines we can walk in.

GOD'S STORYLINE [kingdom of GOD]

THE WORLD'S STORYLINE [kingdoms of this world]

You'll notice one obvious geometric difference when looking at these two storylines: The world's storyline is short. It'd be more accurate to call it a "line segment." It has a definite beginning and a definite ending. When I was in school, we'd have put a dot at each end to show exactly that.

God's storyline, on the other hand, has an arrow on both ends—showing it goes forever in both directions. It is *the* line.

The world's storyline began when sin entered into humanity's experience in the garden of Eden. It started when humanity believed the serpent's lie that a God who loves us would never keep from us something as good as that one restricted fruit. And those of us walking the world's storyline—all of us at some point—have been doubting God's love, goodness, and power ever since.

The world's storyline terminates abruptly, violently, at the end of time when the serpent—along with all those who rejected Jesus as *the path* to living permanently on God's storyline—is locked up once and for all. So, in truth, every second spent lingering on the world's storyline is time wasted on a dead-end path.

As Christians, we know this. We're convinced of it. Yet we continue to struggle to trust God and to stay off the world's path. We desperately want our kids to fully live out their lives on the line that has no beginning and no ending, the line that's energized with the very power of God, the line upon which is found meaning, purpose, hope, and joy for all time. We want our kids to live on God's storyline.

To reinforce the last chapter, the key to continuing to live on God's storyline in front of our kids is to keep talking about God's revelation. It helps to keep thinking about, keep wondering about, keep talking about where God's storyline is headed.

Listen to Paul in Colossians 3:1-4.

> Since, then, you have been raised with Christ, set your hearts on things above, where Christ is seated at the right hand of God. Set your minds on things above, not on earthly things. For you died, and your life is now hidden with Christ in God. When Christ, who is your life, appears, then you also will appear with him in glory.

We want to live on God's storyline because it's the path that runs right into our real world future with God forever. And what wouldn't we give to have our kids join us every day on that path?

The World Is Not Enough

Keeping ourselves and our families on God's path involves understanding enough about the alternate path to want to avoid it—and coming up with a strategy for dealing with the reality of the world all around us. How do we describe the world as we tell God's story to our families?

Let's start by defining it. When used in the Bible, the word *world* can mean a few different things, but we're only interested in one specific idea of world. We're not talking about the world as God's creation. We understand that God created our planet and all living things that reside on it, as well as the stars, the other planets, and the heavens. God called all of those things "good" in the original design. God's creation of the world is one of the first things we know about God's storyline.

We also don't mean *world* in the sense of all the people on the planet Earth. The "world's storyline" isn't meant to communicate "humanity's storyline." God loves people. The best-known verse in the Bible tells us that God loves the world so much that he sent Jesus to earth and gives us the chance to believe in Jesus so we can walk in God's storyline.

So what is the *world*, then? We'll get to some classic biblical definitions in a moment. But let me illustrate what comes to my mind when I think of the *world*. I apologize in advance to the squeamish, but I've spent my life talking to teenagers, and one thing I've discovered is that they love gross illustrations. So here's one for "the world":

Imagine that you, me, and 100 or so of our closest friends squeeze into a very small swimming pool. We barely fit; it's standing room only, shoulder-to-shoulder, torso-to-torso. Now imagine we represent all of the people of the world, and the pool represents the planet, the creation.

After we've been in the pool for about an hour, the water starts to change. We grab a clear cup, scoop up a little sample, hold it up to the light, and notice it's kind of cloudy because of all the epithelia from our dead skin. (Thanks, CSI!) Those skin cells start floating around, kind of reflecting the light and clouding the water. We might look at this container of water and say, "Hey, something's going on with the water. Creation has a problem."

If we waited about four more hours, the water would start to change color, taking on a yellowish tint. An avocado-and-cheese-colored foam might start to float on the surface. Again we scoop out a little water, hold it up to the light, but now we say, "Something's wrong with the planet."

Still we might start looking elsewhere for the source of the problem. We might look at the people in the pool and—based on the fact that the temperature jumps a degree every now and then when somebody makes a funny-looking face—we might say the people in the pool are the cause of the problem in the swimming pool.

Well, the people are part of it. But even they aren't, ultimately, what's going on here. The real problem is a sign on the chain-link fence around the pool that clearly posts the rules: NO DIVING. NO RUNNING. DO NOT URINATE IN THE POOL.

The problem, though, is that over time, those rules have become a little distorted. Somehow the sign has been changed. The words do not in front of the third rule have been rubbed away so it now reads: URINATE IN THE POOL. Therefore the people in the pool are following a distorted belief system.

This is the biblical idea of the world that we're talking about when we discuss the world's storyline. In short, the "world" is a messed-up system of beliefs.

As stated earlier, God originally created the earth and everything in it. And when God was done, he called it all "good." But because of humanity's sin, everything began decaying. The result has been a series of confused, distorted, and out-of-sync systems of belief that humanity willfully and stubbornly followed—in exactly the opposite direction from what God intended.

As parents, our understanding of the world's storyline—and our strategy for responding to it—will deeply affect how we parent our children. Let's look at a few of the stories Christian parents often attempt to live out when it comes to thinking about or integrating with the world.

But before we do that, I want to be clear about one thing: I believe that everyone reading this book wants the best for their kids. We just do. It's how we're wired as parents, and it's also our desire as children of God. We want to do the right thing. We have an instinct to protect. That's a good thing! But sometimes our good instincts can become obstacles to our goal of raising kids who seek God's heart.

Story Strategy One: Isolation from the World

The isolationist attempts to treat the world as if it doesn't exist. The goal is to keep yourself and your family completely walled off from anything that might contain the world's influence. We attempt to protect our children from the world's storyline by completely disconnecting our family from that grid.

The isolation strategy is an understandable response from concerned parents, but it's ultimately motivated by fear. We're afraid of what the world may do to our children. We're afraid God isn't powerful enough in our lives and in the lives of our kids to overcome the influences of the world's messed-up system of beliefs.

Ultimately, building a barrier won't work for two reasons: One, the world always gets around the barrier. We can't keep it out for very long and continue to function in our fallen creation and around other sinful people without being exposed to the world's system.

A second and even bigger reason is that we can't continue to walk in God's storyline if we build a barrier between us and the world. Jesus' Great Commission includes explicit, specific instructions to "go into the world" for the purpose of teaching the gospel and making disciples.

In effect, then, the isolationist can create only a semipermeable membrane. Remember eighth-grade biology? A semipermeable membrane allows substances to flow in but not out. When we attempt to wall out the world, it ends up seeping in despite our best efforts, but we succeed in holding back our own influence as well. By default we receive the world's influence and disobediently refuse to share ours with the world.

Jesus understood this, and Matthew 11:19 tells us what the world said about him: "The Son of Man came eating and drinking, and they say, 'Here is a glutton and a drunkard, a friend of tax collectors and "sinners."' But wisdom is proved right by her actions."

Jesus kept some pretty rough company because he was here to influence those who'd completely bought into the world's storyline. In response some religious people accused Jesus of doing wrong. "But wisdom is proved right by her actions," we're told. Jesus did what was right in reaching out to those lost in the world. His influence was well used by being in their presence.

Earlier in Matthew, Jesus expressly tells his followers that they should stop being isolationists or else they'll lose the influence battle God intends them to win:

> "You are the salt of the earth. But if the salt loses its saltiness, how can it be made salty again? It is no

longer good for anything, except to be thrown out
and trampled by men." (Matthew 5:13)

So many of us have gotten really comfortable living in the saltshaker. We *love* the saltshaker. We love hanging around our salt-crystal buddies, listening to our salt crystal-inspired music, and reading our salt crystal-created books. So we stay in the saltshaker. And then when God lifts up the salt shaker and tries to sprinkle us out into the world to give it a little flavor, to wake it up, to help it come alive, we hang on to that little hole yelling, "No! I don't want to leave! I'm happy inside here! I love my salt-crystal buddies!"

But ultimately we're no good for anything if we don't leave the salt shaker, if we continue fearing that our families will lose the influence battle by being exposed to the world's storyline all around us.

Jesus goes on to say in verses 14-16 of Matthew 5:

"You are the light of the world. A city on a hill cannot be hidden. Neither do people light a lamp and
put it under a bowl. Instead they put it on its stand,
and it gives light to everyone in the house. In the
same way, let your light shine before men, that they
may see your good deeds and praise your Father
in heaven."

Now please understand that I'm not saying we don't need to protect our children, or we don't need to be careful about what we expose our children to at the right ages and stages of life. I'm referring to disobediently isolating our kids, believing that the best way we can help them grow in their faith is by cutting off their interaction from the world.

I'd like to use an example from my own life here. But first let me clearly state that I have no problem with any method of schooling children. I believe that home schooling, Christian schooling, private schooling, and public schooling are all absolutely valid forms of teaching our children.

What motivates the form of schooling we choose, however, could be a concern. Parents who send their kids to public school because it's easy and then fail to engage with them in that experience are making a mistake, I believe. Equally, parents who believe that home-schooling fully protects their kids from the influence of the world are also on the wrong path. It's the motivation behind the method, not the method itself, that's the issue.

My wife, Jade, and I were at a picnic. Of our friends in attendance, some were home-schooling their kids, and others were sending theirs to a private, Christian school. And there we were: The public-school parents. As often happens, the other parents were really surprised to learn we were sending our kids to a public school. As much as I'm involved in ministry, they asked, wouldn't I want to do something else? I tried to be respectful of their point of view, and I hoped they'd be respectful of mine as well.

The kids were all gathered near the corner of the property, and they were playing "getting married." We all thought it was cute, and we started kidding around about making deals with one another for arranged marriages. And then all of a sudden, one of the kids pointed toward the others and shouted, "They're going on a honeymoon, and they're going to kiss with their tongues and have sex!"

All of the parents turned and looked at us—the public-school parents! "How in the world could our kids be talking about that unless your public-school kids taught it to them?" they asked.

Knowing that our kids not only go to public school but also hang around teenagers all the time because we're in youth ministry, it wasn't a far-fetched conclusion that maybe our kids were the ones doing the educating. So my wife ran over to where the kids were, and the home-schooling mom ran over, too.

About five minutes later, two mothers emerged over the hill. My wife had a very pleasant smile on her face. The home school parent looked extremely troubled. And as we sat down around the table, she admitted she just couldn't understand how her kids knew this stuff. She said, "We're so careful. We've tried to monitor what they watch on TV and who they play with."

It wasn't home schooling that failed; the parents' motivation to isolate their kids from the world failed. It doesn't work. The world squeezes its way around our walls, in spite of our careful efforts.

Our daughter, Skye, was a big fan of Disney's High School Musical series, so we were a little mortified in September 2007 when the story broke that naked photos of one of the female stars had shown up on the Internet. We immediately went into isolationist mode for a few minutes, figuring out what it would take to keep that story from reaching our kids.

Just then, as we were still trying to nail down how to keep them from hearing it on the news or elsewhere, Dax and Skye came home from school and told us all about it. They were plugged in—and in ways we just couldn't anticipate. They hadn't seen the photos, but they knew the details. The world had reached them.

It turned into an excellent teaching opportunity, too—one we hadn't anticipated. We talked about how something like this could happen—why people might make the choice to let their pictures be taken while they weren't wearing any clothes—and how they should steer clear of doing something like that. We let them ask us questions. We talked about how our choices can continue to have consequences long after we've made them—because those photos would never go away. Finally, we prayed for the girl and asked God to use the situation for his glory and for the girl to know God through Jesus and find help from him.

When isolation fails and our kids are exposed to things we wish they weren't, we get the opportunity to help them navigate the world around them as it is—and to help them see how that fits into God's storyline.

Story Strategy Two:
Regulating the World's Influence

Another strategy we sometimes use as parents is attempting to regulate the world's influence in certain areas. We kind of draw a dotted line and say, "These things are okay, and in this way you can interact with the world. But in this area, I'm putting up a barrier. We're going to keep the world out at this point of entry."

Of course, putting up barriers and boundaries for our kids is part of parenting. The Youth and Religion study described how important clear barriers are. Kids need them, and we need to put them up.

The problem isn't setting clear limits; the problem comes when we start serving the barriers instead of serving our kids and our intention to help them become men and women who do good, who seek after Christ.

This strategy usually turns parents into "should notters." We find ourselves constantly drawing and redrawing lines for our kids, telling them what they should not do instead of urging our kids in positive directions of going, doing, and becoming. Instead of cheering our kids into action to embrace everything God has made them to be in the world, we find ourselves continually regulating, pulling them back, and telling them what they can't do.

This family story strategy is built on a desire to control our kids, to keep them from (maybe) going the wrong way just in case we aren't there to shadow their every move. We're afraid, again, that if they try things, if they make decisions on their own, then they might fail, might miss out on God's best by doing something improperly—as if they could somehow mess up so badly that they'd lose God's mercy, grace, and loving acceptance.

Another problem with this approach is that it can create rule-following kids who don't understand the big picture of God's story. Kids need boundaries, but they also need to understand the point of those boundaries in order to transfer their faith from your instructions to walking under their own power on God's storyline.

Otherwise they can become like those heartless worshipers described in Isaiah 29:13—

> The Lord says: "These people come near to me with their mouth and honor me with their lips, but their hearts are far from me. Their worship of me is made up only of rules taught by men."

This passage frightens me not only as a follower of Christ, but also as a parent. The idea that I could believe I'm doing it right while my heart is still far away from the heart of God terrifies me. I don't want to be a follower of man-made rules for my own glory—nor do I want to raise kids who do so.

Again, Paul echoes his Old Testament counterpart:

> Since you died with Christ to the basic principles of this world, why, as though you still belonged to it, do you submit to its rules: "Do not handle! Do not taste! Do not touch!"? These are all destined to perish with use, because they are based on human commands and teachings. Such regulations indeed have an appearance of wisdom, with their self-imposed worship, their false humility and their harsh treatment of the body, but they lack any value in restraining sensual indulgence." (Colossians 2:20-23)

In the near term, this strategy may create compliant children who do as we say. But as they mature and realize that the artificial boundaries we created and claimed to be part of God's storyline don't completely align with God's instructions in Scripture, we risk presenting them with such a weak form of the Christian life that they never discover the fullness in following Christ. We also risk leaving them even more vulnerable to the world's influence once those artificial boundaries are removed.

Remember, our hope isn't just to protect our children's innocence for the sake of keeping them innocent. Innocence—not being exposed to harsh or wrong things—isn't the same thing as virtue. Virtue—moral excellence, goodness, righteousness—will come when our kids have been exposed to certain worldly things and then choose to turn away on their own.

Obviously, we don't want our kids to self-regulate before the appropriate age. But when the right time comes along, it's refreshing to see it in action. Skye has started doing it. She'll notice the lyrics to a song on the radio and say, "Can we turn this one off? It's not a good song." We like that she's starting to set up her own barriers based on her understanding of God's story.

One last, unpleasant result of living for regulations and making that our family story strategy for dealing with the world is that it can produce judgmental and spiritually critical kids, as opposed to creating families who walk gratefully in God's grace and mercy with love and honor for the other children on his storyline.

Story Strategy Three: Agreeing with the World

"Well, fine then!" you might be saying now, "I suppose you want us to just let our kids go out and do whatever comes naturally in the world." No, God's Word doesn't allow us to embrace that option either.

Listen to James 4:4: "You adulterous people, don't you know that friendship with the world is hatred toward God? Anyone who chooses to be a friend of the world becomes an enemy of God."

I recently noticed that a two-headed snake sold for $15,000 on eBay. When I was a really young boy, I came into contact with my first two-headed snake at the San Diego Zoo. I was fascinated. After further reading, I found out that it's a common genetic mutation, but you rarely see mature two-headed snakes in the wild because predators typically destroy them before they have a chance to grow. It's only when they're kept in captivity that they're allowed to mature in safety.

Why do they die so young? Because they actually have two brains—two heads controlling one body. So a predator comes along, and one brain says, "Hey, I'm going to go that direction." And the other brain says, "No, we're going in that direction," and—*zap!*—the two brains kind of paralyze the snake. Then a hawk swoops down and gets a two-for-one meal.

Christians who choose to agree with the world want to live both in God's storyline and the world's storyline simultaneously. They attempt to compartmentalize their lives, doing all of their Christian and church stuff on one side and all of their worldly stuff on the other. But they can't operate for long with two brains.

Eventually, one or the other wins out, and it's usually the world's storyline. To maintain both lifestyles, you must decide which one you'll live in today, in this moment...and then in the next. It's exhausting. And soon it becomes paralyzing. In the end, *zap!* A family is devoured by the roaring lion looking for a meal (as described in 1 Peter 5:8).

What it comes down to is fear—but it's opposite from the isolationist's: "What if God's storyline isn't true? What if God is a liar? What if God doesn't do what he says? What if God just wants to keep me from the good things of life?"

Sound familiar? It's the same lie the serpent told Eve in the garden, which led to humanity's distrust of God's Word. And that's how we got onto this worldly storyline in the first place.

Now, as back then, the result of believing the lie, of making the world's storyline our own, is to miss out on life—true life. Jesus put it this way in Matthew 16:25—"For whoever wants to save his life will lose it, but whoever loses his life for me will find it."

And Paul warned us not to be drawn in by the sneaky reasoning of the world: "See to it that no one takes you captive through hollow and deceptive philosophy, which depends on human tradition and the basic principles of this world rather than on Christ." (Colossians 2:8)

We don't want to lead our families down the dead-end storyline of the world, no matter how much more attractive it looks. As Real World Parents, our goal is to model for our children a much more challenging, more vibrant, more active and engaging approach to dealing with the world. We'll explore what that is in the next chapter.

Before you move on to the next chapter, ask yourself these questions:

1. If you grew up in a Christian home, what strategy did your parents attempt to use with you in response to the world's storyline? How effective was that strategy?

2. Which of the three strategies described in the chapter, if any, is closest to your own response to the world's storyline? How effective has that strategy been so far?

Chapter Five

YOUR HOME IS
AN EMBASSY

In the previous chapter, we ruled out three stories we might tell our kids about the world.

We can't effectively isolate ourselves from the world's system and still live on the planet. We can't effectively "should" our children into being grace-filled followers of Jesus by creating a kind of second law to try to keep them from getting too close to the edges of the world. And just giving up and letting our kids try to walk in the world's storyline *and* God's storyline will only lead to heartache, confusion, and division. We can't afford to tell our children a story that implies it's okay to be a friend of the world's system.

So what *do* we do?

We try to follow God's story. Specifically, we try to follow Jesus, who arrived with his own plan for dealing with the world. He came to transform it.

Paul put it this way in his letter to the Romans: "Do not conform any longer to the pattern of this world, but be transformed by the renewing of your mind. Then you will be able to test and approve what God's will is—his good, pleasing and perfect will" (Romans 12:2).

In the English, the translators use two words—*conform* and *transform*—to communicate the idea of this verse. The words are similar in that they both have the root word *form* in them, but they mean different things. We're not to *conform* any longer to the pattern of this world but to be *transformed* by the renewing of our minds.

That phrase tells us there's a pattern to the world, something that repeats over and over and over again. There's nothing new in the world, just its next iteration—another generation following the same old blueprint of serving self.

But the world gets it backward. It looks at Christianity and says, "There's nothing new there. There's nothing fresh going on." And we're tempted to believe it and keep following the world's pattern rather than breaking out and doing something new. But that's what God calls us to—not to conform, but to be transformed by having our minds renewed, made over fresh, changed for the better.

I mentioned in an earlier chapter how much I loved *Star Wars* as a kid. It came out in theaters when I was in third grade, and I saw it then for the first time. I couldn't get enough of it.

I wanted everything that had anything to do with *Star Wars*. In fact, I really wanted a cool *Star Wars* Play-Doh set. It had all three Play-Doh colors. (That's all there was back then. You had to use a color wheel and mix them if you wanted anything other than primary red, blue, and yellow.)

Anyway, it also came with these molds to make the characters. I'd jam some of the yellow Play-Doh—who had time to mix colors?—into the Luke Skywalker mold, push down the plastic, trim off the extra Play-Doh around the edges, and *boom*! Out would pop Luke Skywalker in all his yellow glory.

What started as a yellow blob of Play-Doh had been conformed to the pattern of the image of Luke Skywalker. Awesome! Well, except that it was still just a yellow piece of clay. It looked different, but nothing about its substance had changed.

In this verse in Romans, Paul is telling us, "Become something different! Don't be content to remain the thing you've always been, looking like everyone else around you." In other words, don't pretend that something substantive has changed inside you just because you and your kids spend Sundays in church and you know the Lord's Prayer and you read the Bible. Don't settle for conforming to the world's pattern with a little churchy flavoring thrown in. We need to be *transformed*.

Transformation means going from one thing to something completely new and different and fresh.

The idea of transformation reminds me of a car commercial I saw when I was a kid. It was back when the digital video technique of morphing was just starting to come into vogue. In the commercial, a tiger runs down the road when it melts into a car right in front of our eyes. So cool! As a junior high computer geek who wanted to be Steven Spielberg, it blew me away.

My point, though, is that this commercial depicts a real transformation. It isn't a car painted to look like a tiger. And it isn't a tiger that looks like a car. It's a tiger that *turns into* a car. It's now completely different from what it had been before.

When I read this passage in Romans 12, that's what I imagine. God is calling us to a new purpose, to a new story. We were one thing, and now God wants us to be something else—not something that just *looks* like something else.

The questions to ask are these: *Are our families being transformed? Are we experiencing the everyday reality of walking in a new story?* Our answers matter because walking in that story comes with a new job description for transformed families.

A New Title

Part of our transformation process includes representing the new thing we're becoming (or the new destination we're now moving toward) to the people in the world around us—the ones still stuck fast to the world's perspective. As transforming people, our story should include offering God's transformational gift to the world.

The Bible describes it this way in 2 Corinthians 5:20— "We are therefore Christ's ambassadors, as though God were making his appeal through us." In other words, we're given a whole new title when we choose to walk in God's storyline. We become Christ's ambassadors, his representatives.

Here are two definitions of *ambassador* I found in the dictionary:

> 1. A diplomatic agent of the highest rank accredited to a foreign government or sovereign as the resident representative of his or her own govern-

ment or sovereign or appointed for a special and often temporary diplomatic assignment

2. An authorized representative or messenger[13]

How do these definitions remind you of the Christian life, of living on God's storyline? How could they *not*? The title of ambassador *is* the story of the Christian life; it's the role we fill—together with our families—as we walk through the world without becoming of the world. We are representatives of a country we've never seen, and we're undergoing a process of transformation as we point the world to the source of our hope, the power to be changed—Jesus Christ.

And if we're Christ's ambassadors, that makes our homes embassies for the kingdom of God, doesn't it? Now that's a new story to present and to live in with our children: Our homes are embassies, safe havens, sources of hospitality, places where people can come and learn about our heavenly country, about the King who really saved us and whom we serve and follow.

I remember when I first started thinking seriously about this ambassador concept many years ago, and it was really driven home for me by American Airlines' then brand-new e-ticketing system.

As part of my ministry, I spend a lot of time on airplanes. And when you fly a lot on one airline, as I do on American, the airline assigns you a unique and premium status. Last year I achieved the Executive Platinum status, and I completely bought into all the perks that come with being such a too-frequent flyer.

---

13. http://www.merriam-webster.com/dictionary/ambassador

Your Home Is an Embassy

Before 9/11, this was an even bigger deal because you didn't have to endure nearly as many of the security procedures as "regular" travelers. You could just wave that card and people kind of knew you were special, that you were part of that inner circle. That Platinum Card moved you to the front of the line or to an even better "special" line or past the lines altogether. I loved it!

One day I arrived at the airport early in the morning. I was running slightly behind, but I knew it would be okay because I had the Platinum Card to help me sail through to the gate. But there was a problem: The new e-ticketing system had just been launched, and the check-in area was more chaotic than usual. There were lines where there'd never been lines before.

I walked to the front of the line and flashed my Platinum Card, and the agent said, "I'm sorry, sir, you're going to have to wait at the *end* of the line."

I said, "No, I have a Platinum Card."

And she said, "I know. And you're welcome to wait at the end of the line with the other Platinum Members."

I went to the end of the line feeling bruised. I started talking with the other Platinums (and even a few Golds) about how we'd been treated and how this whole system is messed up and how e-ticketing will never catch on. I started getting angry. I watched the woman behind the counter. She just kept tapping on that computer, and I started thinking to myself, *She doesn't know what she's doing.* I was sure I could've made that computer do more with a blindfold and a hammer than she was doing with her fingers and her eyes wide open!

Seriously, I was furious now. I even worked up this little speech. I thought, *I'm going to give this woman a message like she's never heard before. I'm going to let her know what Frequent Flyer KJW8802 thinks about the way he's been treated on this particular day at American Airlines!* I was actually starting to look forward to letting her have it.

Then all of a sudden I remembered what I'd been preparing to teach about this ambassador stuff—that I don't represent myself, that I'm not a part of the world's system, and that my status doesn't come from American Airlines. Then the battle was on. Inside, I was thinking, *No. No. Don't talk me out of it. I've been wronged! I have a speech!*

But the Holy Spirit just said, "Dude, no. Me. You represent *me*."

Flooded with an overwhelming awareness of how wrong I'd been, I realized again that an ambassador's job description doesn't allow him to represent himself at the expense of the One who appointed him.

So when my turn came, I went up to the counter and, instead of reciting my speech, I said, "Hey, how are you doing today?"

The ticket agent said, "Not very good. You know, everyone is so mad at me. The systems aren't doing what they're supposed to do."

I said, "I'm not mad at you." Now, just 20 seconds earlier that would've been a lie; but at that moment, a transformation had truly occurred in my heart. Then I said, "I'm a minister. When I get on the plane, I'm going to pray that God will give you peace and whatever you need to be able to deal with the challenges of this day."

And she said, with tears in her eyes, "Thank you so much."

Now, I didn't have time to whip out a Four Spiritual Laws booklet and walk her through the plan of salvation. In fact, she may have been a Christian. But in the 10 to 15 seconds that I stood at her counter, I nevertheless served as an ambassador for the kingdom of heaven. I represented my King (instead of myself). I represented my Savior. I represented his way of doing things, not the world's way of doing things. And I remembered once more that this is the story I'm meant to live in every day, not just when I'm standing in line.

Defining Success

How do we do this in our homes? How do we change the story that our families—our children—are walking in? How do we make sure we're not telling them a story that says, "We have to isolate ourselves from the world"? Or a story that's all about rules and what we can't do as Christians? Or telling them Christianity doesn't matter because we're just going to do what we want to do, anyway?

How do we tell a different story?

In part, we're going to do it by changing how we define success in our lives. We're going to come up with new answers to the question: "What makes us successful as a family?"

As a prophet to the nation of Israel, Jeremiah's job included showing people how God's storyline and the world's storyline (the one they were living in) sharply contrast each other. He challenged the Israelites to walk in God's story, the one that defines success so differently from how they were measuring it.

Jeremiah 9:23 says, "This is what the LORD says: 'Let not the wise man boast of his wisdom or the strong man boast of his strength or the rich man boast of his riches.'" In this verse we're clearly told to not boast in these three areas of our lives: Wisdom, strength, and riches.

Take a few minutes, if you would, to really think about that. Then ponder these questions with a little self-reflection:

> Is your family proud of its intellect?
>
> Does your family take pride in achieving a certain level of academic achievement, in how smart you are, in how clever you are, in how creative you are? Is that what you're known for? Is that what you boast about?
>
> Is your family proud of its influence or power or position in the community?
>
> Is your family proud of its wealth?

Your children's sense of spiritual well-being begins with your definition of success. If, as a family, you define success according to wealth, intellect, and status, that tells your kids a lot about what story you believe you're living in.

Whatever you're proud of—what you're trying to make known about your family—impacts your kids' understanding of the importance of God's story. Even if we never talk about money or worldly success and say instead that God's way is the most important one, our kids are canny. They catch the truth from watching how we live and by noticing the story that our actions and attitudes are telling.

The following set of self-analysis or family-analysis questions will help you think about what your family is truly valuing or hoping in or putting their security in. Try to answer them honestly.

WHAT DO YOU REWARD?

What in your household most readily gets the full attention of Mom or Dad? What action is most likely to provoke an encouraging word? Praise from you is a gift. *At what moments or in response to what achievements are you most likely to give praise? What you reward reveals what you value.*

WHAT OR WHOM DO YOU ADMIRE?

Our kids notice the things we esteem. They size up the people we admire. They examine our heroes and role models and decide, on some level, "So *that's* what success looks like. They think, *This is Mom's idea of what a woman should look like,* or *This is Dad's idea of what a real man is. I should be like that. Whom do you admire?*

WHAT DO YOU FINANCIALLY SUPPORT?

Your kids also notice what you do and don't spend your money on, even if you don't share with them how you specifically designate your savings, spending, and giving. They catch on to where you put your treasure and what your heart truly values.

I was talking about this issue with a youth pastor in North Carolina as we were checking into a hotel. The woman who was checking us in almost started crying as we talked.

I said, "Ma'am, are you okay?"

She said, "Excuse me for eavesdropping. What you were talking about caught my attention. I'm having trouble in my family right now, and what you just said about what we support as parents really hit me. I complain about every penny I have to pay the church for a youth group activity. But when it comes to sports, I write checks without any problem whatsoever. And I just realized that I'm teaching my kids that God isn't the most important thing in our lives."

I couldn't have said it better myself.

Jeremiah used the word *boast*. I like to talk about what we're *known for*, what our families are known for. Does what we're known for in the areas of our money, our attention, and our esteem show that we're living in God's story as ambassadors of Jesus—or that we're living in the world's story as ambassadors of ourselves?

In the next verse, Jeremiah tells us what God says we can and should boast about: "But let him who boasts boast about this: that he understands and knows me, that I am the LORD, who exercises kindness, justice and righteousness on earth, for in these I delight." (9:24)

God wanted the Israelites to be content with understanding and knowing God more than money, status, or strength. And God wants the same for our families.

Asking Hard Questions Together

This exercise might not be a good fit for every family, but we've put together a series of questions you can use with your spouse or kids to get your family asking some hard questions about what storyline you're living in. It's one thing to talk together about living in God's storyline; it's quite another to really evaluate your words, actions, and attitudes and see if there's any evidence in your lives that you're on God's path.

First, sit down with your family. (Note: This may be an unusual thing for you to do. If it's too wild a departure from the way you usually operate when you're having a family conversation in the same room, then maybe you could talk to your kids individually before trying to pull them all together. But sit down with your family members and be real with them.)

Second, tell them you don't have all the answers, but you want to lead them in deeper walks in the storyline of God. Be open about your own struggles with that idea. The fact that you tell them you don't always know what's going on may very well make an impact on them.

Next, pray with your family, if that doesn't seem too awkward. Ask God to help you see things you've been missing. Then read aloud the verses we've just covered—Jeremiah 9:23-24. Ask your family straight up: "Do we define success more by the world's storyline or God's storyline?"

You may find some of the following questions helpful in getting the conversation rolling:

> Is our family known for understanding and knowing God?

> How many of our family conversations naturally center on our worship and love of God?

> Do our neighbors notice that our relationships with God are a big deal to us?

> Is our family known for kindness?

> Is our family generous toward others?

> Do we use words to show love to and comfort others?

> Do we serve people in our neighborhood?

> Is our home a place for hospitality in our community?

Are we known as a family who cares about justice and does the right thing?

Do we stand up for those whom others look down upon?

Do we do what's right even when it costs us?

Are we seen as being trustworthy and honest?

Are we known for respecting authority?

Now invite your family to brainstorm about ways you could grow in these areas. Then pray together and ask God to help you do that.

According to James 4, what increases the power of praying together (for help to be the kind of family God wants us to be) is that God gives grace to the humble. Prayer is an act of humility. When we ask God for help, we unleash God's grace into our lives.

Finally, make a plan to go out and implement some of these new ideas. This might not be easy. Some of the things your family comes up with might feel awkward, especially at first. Talk about them as you go along to see if they're a good fit for who you are as a family or if there might be better ways to live God's story in your community.

But don't just give up, either. Find what works for you. Find something that feels natural to your mix of personalities, your strengths as a family. You don't need to force it, especially if you have older kids who refuse to participate. That's okay. Even if they don't come along, they'll notice that these things are important to you. It will matter to them in the long run.

You don't want your kids to serve God or others in insincere ways. Remember, you're the lead ambassador in your home. Therefore, you must continue to do those things and give your kids the cognitive autonomy they need to make this stuff their own as well. That will allow them to join in and follow in that storyline as God works on their hearts and brings them into that experience.

In the next few chapters, we'll get more specific about how we can help our kids become worthy ambassadors for Christ in the areas of demonstrating wisdom, making good decisions, evaluating entertainment, and living with hope for the end of the story.

Before you move on to the next chapter, ask yourself these questions:

1. Do the Christians in your family believe they're essentially different from unbelievers (i.e., strangers to the false story the world is telling)?

2. What happens within the walls of your home—your embassy in a foreign land called Earth—that's different from what happens outside of the walls of your home?

3. What's one area where you could help your family redefine "success" by the standards of God's story instead of by the standards of the world's storyline?

Chapter Six

DEMONSTRATING WISDOM

The heart of God's story of the universe is found in his Son. Jesus. As parents, we can understand that, can't we? In many ways, the heart of our personal stories has a lot to do with our kids. They're the focus of so much of our time and energy, and certainly our thoughts and emotions. We love our kids.

And as we mentioned in the last two chapters, that love can sometimes drive us to reactions both positive and negative. Positively, it can motivate us to help them figure out how to navigate as people of faith in God's story while living in a culture saturated in sin. Negatively, we can shelter and legislate our children into a form of religion that doesn't resemble a healthy relationship with Jesus.

Being spiritually successful is an incredibly difficult thing to do on our own. So it's no wonder we feel helpless about our children's chances of succeeding. Their only hope to make it, really, is to navigate within the wisdom of God. That's what this chapter is about—how to demonstrate and impart wisdom to our kids for navigating the world.

God's wisdom—the wisdom of his Word—is so very practical. It helps us see the world as it is, not as we wish it were. But that's where our other instinct comes from—the one that wants to hold the world back, to lock the door and keep our kids away from it.

We feel sad and frustrated when we look around and see how the world has warped God's creation, how God's design has been abused and destroyed by human sin. And then we can get so angry or bitter or just plain exhausted that we just want to put up a wall and keep it all out. But we know that doesn't work.

So Jesus shows us another path. God sent us the Son he loves so much—not only to die, but also to *live* in the heart of the world. And Jesus walked through the world shining a bright light to call all people to his Father. How did Jesus do it? How can our kids do it?

For one thing, Jesus saw life the way God sees life: He walked in the world with wisdom.

Jesus Grew in Wisdom?

It seems only right for parents to want their children to walk the way Jesus walked in human form, to grow as Jesus grew. So how did he grow? One passage—one sentence, really—tells all we know regarding that part of the story, the part when Jesus was growing up (before John the Baptist poured water from the Jordan River over Jesus' head, and God spoke from heaven saying he loves Jesus).

Here's the line: "And Jesus grew in wisdom and stature, and in favor with God and men" (Luke 2:52).

That sentence used to baffle me a little when I first took this passage seriously. I mean, I understood the "stature" part: Jesus grew physically. I understood that God the Father was well pleased with Jesus. And I understood that Jesus grew in favor with the people: They liked him. Jesus handled himself well in social situations and lived in peace and harmony with others. Those parts all made perfect sense.

But that word *wisdom* was more mysterious. I understood spiritual growth as having to do with reading the Bible, praying, going to church, maybe tithing, maybe evangelizing. But how do you grow in wisdom? That wasn't nearly as central to our church-speak concerning growth. It wasn't included in the basics of discipleship, in my experience.

So I was drawn into understanding more about wisdom. I mean, if Jesus grew in wisdom as a kid, then I wanted to do that, too. And now I want to know how to help my own kids grow wise. Over time I realized that growing in wisdom involves powerful ideas that can help us walk in God's story more effectively. In fact, wisdom helps us live the practical, mundane, everyday moments of our lives from a spiritual perspective.

One of the first things to understand about wisdom is where it comes from, and it starts here: "The fear of the LORD is the beginning of wisdom, and knowledge of the Holy One is understanding" (Proverbs 9:10).

The first startling thing about wisdom is that it begins with fear. If we could somehow stand in the presence of God, I believe we'd know exactly what this means. God's power is too great—and too deadly—to be received by a human being with anything but rigid terror. It would be terrifying.

And standing there scared to death, we'd do nothing—not a thing—that God didn't specifically tell us to do because we'd be too afraid to take any initiative. God's way would be the only way, or we wouldn't move.

And that would be the beginning of being a wise person.

The second phrase in the wisdom passage says that to know God, the Holy One, is to have understanding. Remember the National Study of Youth and Religion findings about growing spiritually healthy kids? One of the three most significant things kids need is an understanding of what the boundaries are and why they exist. And the key to "understanding" in the deepest and most meaningful sense is knowing God.

So we'd realize that growing in wisdom—and helping our kids grow wise—starts with a healthy fear of God that provokes us to do things God's way, and we grow to better understand God's way as we get to know him.

Hebrew scholars tell us that *hokma*, the word for wisdom, literally means "skill" or "expertise." It's the same word used in Exodus to describe the magicians Pharaoh commanded to replicate the miracles of Moses. They had *hokma*—skill or expertise in doing those things. The word is also used to describe the artisans and craftsmen who constructed the tabernacle.

So when we start talking about *hokma* in Proverbs and the other wisdom literature of the Bible, it makes sense to me to define it this way: "Wisdom is a deep, practical understanding of what God is up to in the world so we can walk in his storyline."

If *hokma* really means "skill or expertise," then it should mean "skill at living life" or "expertise at everyday existence" when applied to our lives. In other words, wisdom is the skill of living well. And if we're living well—if we're making good, practical choices in every area of life—then we're walking in God's storyline.

And that just seems logical, doesn't it? Who'd know better about how a high-performance sports car is intended to run than the folks who designed and built the car? If you want to know the best possible way to repair, maintain, and operate your high-performance sports car, you should really ask them. It's their design, right? And they recorded the most important points of knowledge in the owner's manual.

And who'd know better about how life is designed to operate than the God who designed and built it from the ground up? In addition to God being God—which should be a little scary to us—he's also the Designer, Builder, Maintainer, and Life-giver. If you want real answers, the Author of life is the ultimate source for everyday wisdom of every kind.

Finding Wisdom—and Passing It On

Kids get wisdom—wisdom that sticks, wisdom that changes how they operate every day, wisdom that gives them practical skills for living—from two main sources.

The first way kids acquire wisdom is from direct exposure to their environment. If a child puts his hand on a hot stove and burns his hand, then chances are good he won't do it the next time he's near the stove.

But that's not the best way to learn, is it? If that were the only way to acquire wisdom, then the world would be full of maimed, burned, scratched, and scarred people. That's learning wisdom the hard way, and we don't want our kids to spend their lives being taught primarily by Mr. Pain.

There's another, better way for kids to acquire wisdom, and that's through a human mediator—someone who acts as a go-between, an interface between our interior world and the exterior world beyond our senses.

An example of this might be a parent taking a child's hand and holding it close to the stove while saying, "Hot! Hot!" The parent might then take the child to a lit candle and hold his little hand close to the flame—but far enough away to keep him from getting burned—and say again, "Hot!" Next, the parent could do the same thing with a glowing red charcoal from the grill on the patio. Very soon, the child will have an understanding of what "Hot!" means.

The mediator (parent) in this case helped the child gain wisdom through nearly direct exposure to the environment but in a controlled and safe(r) setting.

But it's even better than that. The child has learned not only the life skill (wisdom) of not touching stoves, candles, and charcoals but also to be wary of everything hot that glows red. In the future he'll wisely be on the lookout for hot things and, more specifically, red, glowing hot things.

Building on that, he might soon pick up the idea that different things in the environment can share similar properties. Since different kinds of things can be hot, he'll start to notice that different kinds of things can also be hard or soft or cold. Or he might pick up that the way to approach something new and unusual is cautiously, slowly. As he starts to apply these life skills to the rest of his environment, he eventually approaches strange dogs and other potentially new and harmful objects more carefully—all because someone showed him the stove and the candle and the charcoal were "Hot!"

Such a positive end result makes wisdom taught intentionally and effectively through a human mediator—usually you, the parent—exponentially better than wisdom taught through hard-knock experience with the environment alone.

Are you catching the big idea here? As the human mediator of wisdom in your child's life, your role is far more significant than I'm guessing you usually give yourself credit for. Every bit of wisdom you can give to your kids—real, biblical wisdom based on an understanding of God and his world—has the potential to double and triple itself as your child applies it across the full spectrum of the environment.

You've heard it before, but it's especially true with wisdom: *You can make a huge difference in your kids' lives by being not only wise, but also intentional about teaching wisdom to your children.* You don't need to wait for them to bang into the walls and bruise themselves before you show them the door. If you have wisdom to give, then sharing it with your kids is a gift that will keep unfolding itself throughout their lives—if they'll receive it from you.

Wise Ambassadors

Connecting with our earlier chapter about being Christ's ambassadors and making our homes embassies of his kingdom, we see another essential element to our role in God's story: *Ambassadors require lots of wisdom to do their jobs well.*

They have to know how to live appropriately in foreign countries, how to live considerately of those lands' cultures without being needlessly offensive. But they also have to know how to represent the culture of the home kingdom honestly and faithfully. They have to do both without selling out their king by compromising his standards while they're living in foreign lands.

That takes wisdom and diplomacy. That takes knowing how to negotiate the things of life in their environment, in the world around them. We want our kids to become wise ambassadors for their home country of heaven while living their everyday lives in the world and as part of the culture of their generation.

That kind of wisdom requires understanding. We're back to the National Study of Youth and Religion again. It doesn't take wisdom to stay within the boundaries or simply follow a list of dos and don'ts. But our kids need lots of wisdom to apply the truth of the Bible to the varied situations of their lives. That's when it's vital that our children understand the *reasons* for those boundaries so they can apply those reasons to the daily contexts of their environments.

Does that sound like compromise? It shouldn't. We're not saying that truth or obedience to God is context-sensitive. We're not suggesting that ethics or morality is situational. What we're saying is that sometimes kids need wisdom to make the best choices, and we can't possibly provide them with enough rules to cover every scenario. But by helping them to understand the motives behind our rules, the wisdom our instructions are built on, they'll be able to adjust when the scenario changes to something unfamiliar.

Here's a ridiculous example. You've told your children not to run near the pool. Of course, your reason for saying so is because you want them to be safe; you don't want them to slip and fall. But if your children were being chased by other children with knives, then you would hope they'd use wisdom to reason, *The danger of the knife-wielding children is greater than the danger of the pool. I believe I shall run!* You wouldn't want them to conclude, *The rule is "No running," so I'll follow the rule while getting stabbed.*

This example demonstrates why you can teach the application of wisdom to only one or two people at a time. You can teach a large group what the Bible says about wisdom, but you can't give both Larry and Darrell the same blanket wisdom for particular situations in their separate lives. Wisdom isn't about the bottom line; it's about the application of bottom-line truth to a fluid environment.

That's why your parenting of your children matters so deeply. You know God's Word, and you know your kids. You want to apply God's absolute truth to their everyday changing circumstances—and help them figure out how to do the same thing for themselves as they represent the culture of heaven from within the culture of the world.

Of course, that means you and I have to *know* God's Word and be growing wise, just as Jesus did. Indeed the most effective way to teach wisdom is to demonstrate wisdom. It's okay if you don't always feel wise; it's not too late. Wisdom is still available to you through the study of God's Word, through asking God for it (see James 1:5), and through the wise teachers in your life. Don't give up—your kids really need your wise perspective (even if they don't know they need it).

Let me put it another way: Yoda couldn't teach Luke how to use the Force if Yoda didn't know how to use the Force. Mr. Miyagi couldn't teach Daniel-san to master karate if Mr. Miyagi didn't know how to use karate. And we cannot teach our kids how to skillfully walk in God's story with biblical wisdom if we don't take practicing it very seriously.

In the next chapter, we'll look at ways we can help our kids apply God's wisdom to the specific skills of making good decisions.

Before you move on to the next chapter, ask yourself these questions:

1. How would you define the word *wisdom* after reading this chapter?

2. What active steps have you taken to get wisdom and make wise choices in your life? What other ways of seeking and finding wisdom could you embrace?

3. After reading this chapter, why would you say you're uniquely qualified to pass on wisdom to your children? Why are you a better option for this task than anyone else?

4. In what areas of life do you hope to see your child increase in wisdom the most?

Chapter Seven

TURNING PAGES: TEACHING DECISION MAKING

A significant stage of childhood development is becoming convinced in every area of life that our choices have consequences—and that we're responsible for those consequences.

But overprotective parents can sometimes delay this experience for their kids by making all of their choices for them or quickly "fixing" all of their wrong choices so they never have to suffer the natural outcomes of those decisions.

We do it out of love—albeit a loving reaction to the fear we feel for them. We are unconvinced that our kids are capable of doing things on their own. But they *will* grow up! It's inevitable. And we have the opportunity to help them grow in wisdom. How can we begin to give them the necessary tools now so that as they make bigger and bigger decisions, they'll experience the best possible outcomes we could hope for them?

By this point in the book, you have a pretty good idea that I'm going to tell you it has a lot to do with how we model Real World decision making in front of our children. Of course, they might notice what choices we make—from what we wear to work every day to what car we buy to whether or not they're allowed to stay out late—but how often do we let them walk through the process we use to arrive at those choices?

You and I might not even realize all of the factors that play into our decisions every day. We just know it's time to make the next one. But we do, generally, have some kind of process, and we *can* learn to articulate it. For our kids' sake, it will be worth the effort.

For instance, picture this exchange:

"Mom, can I go over to Sarah's house for a sleepover tonight?"

"No."

"Why not?"

"Because I said so. Please have a good attitude about this."

Of course, this parent is well within the framework of good parenting to simply lay down the law and leave it up to the child to work through the submission issues that come with being a person under authority and to figure out how to handle disappointment with a right attitude. Sometimes this response is acceptable. However, it doesn't take advantage of the potential learning opportunity to show our kids how we arrive at our decisions—not only so they understand we're not heartless killjoys out to destroy their social lives, but also so they see how we work from step A to B to C in arriving at a decision that impacts them directly. In other words, they'll be paying the closest attention to our decision-making model when what they want is at stake.

So the conversation could also go like this:

"Mom, can I go over to Sarah's house for a sleepover tonight?"

"No."

"Why not?"

"I know you have a good time with Sarah, and I know you're old enough to go to sleepovers with your friends. Usually, it would be okay. However, what I remember from past sleepovers is that you tend to come home really tired because you haven't slept much. On top of that, I've noticed you seem to be catching the cold your brother had. We're leaving early to go to your grandma's house the day after tomorrow, and I really don't want you to get sick or be too worn out to enjoy the time with your cousins."

Your daughter still might not like your call on this one—and as the "authority," you certainly didn't owe her the explanation.

But at the very least, you've modeled for her the ability to think ahead, to connect events and their consequences, and to make value judgments between one event and another.

Decisions Every Day

During our children's lifetimes, they'll make thousands—maybe millions—of decisions. Those choices will come in every shape and size, and they'll require a variety of strategies. Our hope as Real World Parents is to give them a few tools regarding how to go about making decisions *now*—when the stakes are lower and we're here to back them up—before they get to a point in their lives where the clock is ticking, and they're deciding between cutting the blue wire and the red wire in order to save the world from a global thermonuclear device.

Okay, so they probably won't have to stop a terrorist attack at a moment's notice. But their choices will still have far-flung consequences. Some of the choices your grandparents made still impact you today. Everyone makes life-altering choices about things such as spouses, colleges, careers, and how to respond to temptations, not to mention decisions made in agreement with God's larger story—his big-R reality—and those made in spite of it.

As mentioned a few paragraphs ago, one of the biggest truths we want to model for and enforce with our kids is that they're responsible for their choices—and that their choices have consequences. Even things we don't always regard as "decisions" are exactly that.

Here's a typical (and hopefully unconscious) process that's nearly universal to children: *Should I go in for dinner right away when I hear Dad calling me? What are my options, and what will the consequences be? If I go right away, there will be no drama. If I wait five minutes, he'll call me again. Still no drama. If I wait 10 minutes, he'll be unhappy, but he won't punish me. If I wait 15 minutes, I'll get both the lecture and some form of punishment. I'll choose to wait 10 minutes.*

In truth, we've been teaching our kids to make decisions on their own ever since we started asking them to do things and delivering our own parent-made consequences in response to their actions. Many of us have responded to good parenting resources by doing that even more intentionally, using the language of choices and consequences with our kids from a very small age.

Hopefully, our kids have started to understand that their choices lead to specific consequences with us. And hopefully we're being intentional enough to tell them we're simply imitating how God works in his story of the universe. As we do with our own kids, God asks the children he loves to obey him in every area of their lives. When we don't, when we willfully disobey God, he disciplines his children. (See Hebrews 12.)

That discipline is the loving (though painful) correction of a dad, but we're careful to distinguish between that and punishment for our sins. As followers of Jesus, our sins are paid for and forgiven. Therefore, God's discipline is intended to provide a painful enough consequence to bring us back into his arms and onto his chosen path for us.

There's also the sense that God has designed the universe to work according to a specific set of standards that provide natural consequences for our choices. (Remember the definition of *wisdom*?) If I were to jump from an airplane without a parachute, the fall to my death wouldn't be God's punishment for my wrong choice. My grisly demise would simply be the consequence of ignoring that part of God's design that includes gravity and the fact that people are denser than air.

If I chose to jump *with* a parachute and pulled the ripcord at the right moment, the consequence of floating safely to the ground would also be in line with God's design for the universe in regard to the laws of physics.

Honestly, most of us (even our kids) understand that big idea of suffering as a consequence of making wrong moral choices—even if we're still convincing ourselves by testing the limits.

The choices that are most difficult—the ones that can sometimes paralyze our children and us—are the ones between two seemingly equal moral choices. In other words, what's the "best" choice? What's the better of these two options? Or even, what's God's will for my life? In that vein, we've put together five basic principles for using wisdom to make those kinds of decisions.

Helping your kids learn to implement these steps into their decision making will help them become more natural and comfortable decision makers as their choices get more consequential in the coming years.

Five Steps for Making Great Decisions

1. SLOW DOWN!

The enemy of good decisions is often—not always, but often—our own impulsiveness. Every good salesperson knows that customers who say, "Give me a day to think it over" are unlikely to come back the next day and put money down. Time almost always brings more wisdom.

Proverbs 19:2 reads, "It is not good to have zeal without knowledge, nor to be hasty and miss the way."

Why do we so often make decisions quickly? There are several possible reasons. Sometimes we just push the button for the thing that seems most obvious to us at first glance. Often that instinctive choice is the right one, but not often enough.

Other times we decide quickly because we know that if we take any time to think about it, we'll talk ourselves out of doing something we know is wrong—but we want to do it anyway. This one is just pure foolishness. Proverbs describes it as "rushing in" to wrongdoing, and it's the exact reason we need to hit the pause button on finalizing our choices until the impulse passes, and we're thinking with clear heads again.

Another reason we sometimes hurry our decisions is that it feels like productivity, like we're getting something done. Living with an unresolved decision can create a kind of tension. It can feel uncomfortable. But we want our kids to become comfortable with maintaining that discomfort long enough to make the right choices.

When talking through decisions with your kids—whether they're your choices to make or theirs—demonstrate the patience to wait and think before pulling the trigger.

2. GATHER INFORMATION

We live in the information age. Never before have we had immediate access to so many facts, figures, prices, reviews, opinions, and statistics. We have very few excuses for not knowing the scores before we make our best choices.

Many of us have had an experience like this one: A friend of mine was in the market for a TV. He was buying something else at Best Buy, saw a great deal on a TV, and immediately bought it. While driving home, he started second-guessing the impulse and wishing he'd waited. (See Step 1.)

He decided it wasn't too late to gather information. When he arrived home, and before he took the TV out of his car, he jumped on Amazon.com and started reading the reviews for that specific TV model. More than half of them described the TV blinking out after about a month and told sad stories of trying to get it repaired. No wonder it was such a good deal!

My friend drove straight back to the store and got his money refunded.

Proverbs 18:17 tells us, "The first to present his case seems right, till another comes forward and questions him."

If we've heard only one perspective or one side of the story, then we don't have enough information to make a good decision. Sometimes, the choice requires actually talking and listening to people, as opposed to merely reading reviews on the Internet. Proverbs also repeatedly encourages us to go out and seek wise counsel from people who know what they're talking about.

One way we can help our kids to challenge their own decision-making processes when they're considering purchases, joining extracurricular teams, or going on dates is to ask about their research. *Is there any way they could gather a little more information? Could they talk to one or two people who've been on that team and ask them about the coach or the experience? Does the person they'd like to go out with have any friends (or former dates) they could grill?*

It's a Real World habit all of us can do—but especially our kids.

3. QUESTION YOUR MOTIVES

As we all know, one thing that sometimes causes decision making to become so tricky is that our reasons for wanting one option over the other get a little slippery. Remember when King David wrote that God desires truth in the inner parts (Psalm 51:6)? That's harder than it looks on paper. You and your kids are great at talking yourselves into things while you hide from the truth about what you really want. (And I know you are, because I am, too.)

Consider a high school student who's been planning to attend a particular college for a long time. It's a good school. She's done all her research. The financial aid options have been explored. The school has an excellent art program that she's interested in exploring.

Then one day she announces she's thinking about going to a different school. It's closer to home, but it doesn't offer the major she was interested in pursuing at the other school. You soon learn that the guy she's been dating for a month (!) is going to this college next year. While she's listing all the great things about this school—and some of them may actually be better than the first school—you know her real motive is to be closer to this guy.

Does telling ourselves the truth about our motives make our choices easier? Not necessarily, but at least we're having honest conversations. Help your children learn to say right out loud why they like both of the options in front of them. Even with small things, try to encourage the habit: "What do you think you'd like about going swimming? And what would be good about going to the movie?" Or, later in life, "What do you think would be good about being on the track team? Going out for wrestling? Keeping your part-time job?"

Stating the perceived benefits of each option out loud can often bring to light hidden motives that we didn't even realize were there.

Of course, if in telling ourselves the truth about our motives we discover what we really want is to move closer to some sinful experience, then that can help us rule out that option—or at least know we're really making a choice between serving our flesh and serving God.

4. GET HELP FROM GOD

Proverbs 21:30 tells us, "There is no wisdom, no insight, no plan that can succeed against the Lord."

Do your kids see you turning to God for help with big and small decisions in your life? Do they see you asking for God's wisdom, the wisdom he promised to give away for free in James 1:5? Do they see you looking into God's Word for help in making hard choices—and making changes based on what the Bible teaches?

We're calling this Step 4, but that doesn't mean it's the least important step to show your kids. Many decisions are made that much easier by being willing to submit our timing (Step 1), knowledge (Step 2), and motives (Step 3) to God's will as expressed in the Bible.

Some decision-making questions that should become second nature to us: *Do any of my options violate God's instructions in his Word? Would I have to disobey my parents, tell a lie, or violate any of my other biblical convictions to do this? If so, that should make the decision for me.*

Am I doing this only to avoid hard work, a prior commitment, or a responsibility to a friendship? Then I should seriously question saying yes to this decision.

In doing this, will I be able to continue loving God with all of my heart, soul, mind, and body and also love others as I love myself? Will I be able to honor Christ and serve as his ambassador if I make this choice? If not, then that should help eliminate the choice, as well.

Help your kids see how you use God's Word to eliminate certain choices and discover new ones, as well as how you ask God for help in making the best choices possible.

5. COMMIT YOUR DECISION TO THE LORD—AND CHOOSE!

There's a continuum of decision making between those of us who decide things impulsively—to our harm—and those of us who put off deciding things for too long—also to our detriment. We want to help our children find the middle part of that line where they take the time to weigh important choices but don't get stuck in the paralyzing fear of making the wrong choice.

Proverbs 16:3 makes us a promise: "Commit to the Lord whatever you do, and your plans will succeed." That verse is frequently quoted when people are making hard choices, but I don't believe it's some kind of magical formula for forcing God to make all my plans work out exactly as I have them lined up in my head.

Instead I'm convinced God cannot fail. God *will not fail*. If my plans are God's—and I'm available to be changed, reinforced, altered, enhanced, and remolded by God—then those plans will succeed. After all, you've given the plans to God, right? I don't view this as a cheat to get the verse to say something it doesn't. I mean to say it gives me the freedom to make choices without being afraid I'm somehow going to mess up the universe. God is so much bigger than any choice I make between two seemingly pretty good options.

I haven't read this book by Kevin DeYoung yet, but I love the title: *Just Do Something: A Liberating Approach to Finding God's Will or How to Make a Decision without Dreams, Visions, Fleeces, Impressions, Open Doors, Random Bible Verses, Casting Lots, Liver Shivers, Writing in the Sky, Etc.* There's a whole lesson in the title alone!

As parents, especially, we should be concerned with teaching our kids to take decision making seriously because decisions do have serious consequences. But we should also model for them the confidence we have in God that he's big enough to use our good-willed, obedient, and honest decisions for his glory. Let's not show our kids how to dread failed decisions but rather how to freely make the best ones we can and keep going.

Paul writes it this way in Colossians 3:17—"And whatever you do, whether in word or deed, do it all in the name of the Lord Jesus, giving thanks to God the Father through him."

Once you've waited, gathered info, questioned your motives, asked God for wisdom, and checked your options against the part of God's will revealed in his story—go for it! Help your kids go for it, too, and be prepared to learn from the results.

As we'll see in the next chapter, the best decisions often follow the worst ones. We cannot be afraid to see our kids fail sometimes. It's an essential part of growing up and growing wise. The key is to help them fail successfully.

Before you move on to the next chapter, ask yourself these questions:

1. After reading this chapter, which of the five aspects of making good decisions do you need to practice the most? How specifically could you practice that aspect of decision making when next faced with a decision?

2. How open are you with your kids about your decision-making process? Do they notice when you struggle with a hard decision? Do they get a chance to hear or understand the reasoning behind the choices you make?

Chapter Eight

FAILING IN GOD'S STORYLINE

O ur family loves to watch the final rounds of the National Geographic Bee every year. Not only is it educational; it's high drama!

If you follow the Bee, have you noticed during the last decade or two how many of the winners have been home schoolers? That's no coincidence. As I mentioned in a previous chapter, my own kids go to a great public school, and I believe every schooling option is valid if parents are engaged and their motives are right. And parents with the time, skills, and interest to seriously focus on their children's education at home often succeed in producing bright, well-focused, high-achieving students.

The winner of the first-ever National Geographic Bee (called the National Geography Bee in 1989) was an eighth-grader named Jack Staddon who was educated in a six-person Seventh-day Adventist school in Kansas. Maybe that's why I love what he said after winning the competition by correctly naming *altiplano* (which, as we all know, is the flat intermountain area located at 10,000 feet in the central Andes).

Jack said, "It's nice to win, but even if I lost, I'd thank the Lord anyway. It gives you practice in knowing how to fail."

I guess it's easy for the winner to say that, but Jack's answer showed enormous wisdom for a high-achieving student. (Note: I recently corresponded with him, and Jack still feels the same way.) And that kind of wisdom you can easily give your own kids if you're willing to help them fail productively.

Yes, you read that correctly. I did write, FAIL PRODUCTIVELY. Let me explain.

Several years ago, a home school group in our area asked me to speak to their kids on the issue of facing their fears. When the contact person called me, she said many of the children in the group were getting ready for college and were kind of afraid. When the home school moms asked how I'd learned to overcome *my* fears, I told them it was easy: I'd grown up in public school. They didn't think that was very funny. But I did tell them that my parents had taught me how to fail productively, and that I could share that idea with their kids, too.

Actually I thought it was a great topic for these achievement-focused kids. One thing that's true of any bright student is that nearly every aspect of life can become about *mastery*. I use that word intentionally. In our education-rich society, smart, talented students have a wide range of academic sub-jects, sports, and extracurricular activities to choose from. It only makes sense that they'd focus on the ones they're good at doing.

As they get closer to high school graduation and start thinking about acquiring scholarship money from good col-leges, the pressure builds to create applications crammed with details about their sparkling successes to help them compete with all of those other smart, talented, gifted, insightful kids out there.

As parents, teachers, and youth workers, we can unwit-tingly join forces to deliver a high-pressure message of "don't fail." In many ways we say to our kids, "Don't blow it. Your whole future is at stake. Don't waste time on anything you're merely passionate about. Focus solely on what you excel in— and be the best at it. You don't have time to make mistakes right now. You must succeed."

We can deliver a similar message as the church—but often with far less subtlety—when we define *success* for Christians as having high-performance Bible knowledge, active church involvement, and an under-the-radar record of sin while at the same time achieving success academically, athletically, or in other areas.

I can tell you from reading the stats and talking to youth and youth leaders: *Our kids are stressed out about success and failure.* And we haven't even talked about the most immedi-ate pressures they face—to live up to the expectations of their peer groups and culture. Body-image choices. Clothes. Social-networking standards. Personal taste snobbery—judging each other by the music, movies, actors, and fashion accessories we prefer. Even at that level, the message is as it's always been: "If you can't achieve, then at least don't stand out. Don't fail.

Don't be the joke." Teens today feel as though they can't fail. The consequences appear to be too great a price to pay.

But here's the problem with living with such high stakes for failing: *Failure is essential to success in every arena of life.* You simply cannot be great at anything if you haven't experienced some measure of failure. That's a statement that still rings false in our ears to some degree, even in spite of all the historical evidence piling up around us.

You've heard the dusty old illustrations about how Thomas Edison failed repeatedly before, during, and after creating his world-changing inventions. He used up decades and fortunes on ideas that never got off the ground while on his way to bringing to life the ones we all know about today.

And what baseball fan hasn't noticed that home run kings seem to always hold strikeout records? In a game where the best players in the world succeed in hitting the ball only 30 percent of the time, the ones who hit it the farthest make contact even less often—and in a most frustrating, embarrassing way.

We know those things, but parents can still get panicky at the thought of their kids failing in noticeable ways. Our natural instinct is to protect them from failing at anything—classes, athletics, relationships, even the expectations of Christian friends.

Let's take a minute to examine what motivates that fear of failure and then talk about how to help our kids fail successfully.

What Are We Afraid Of?

When I talk about learning to fail successfully or productively, I don't mean to be glib about it. Failure hurts! It almost always represents a loss on some level. And it's often expensive in terms of time, money, energy, or focus. Failure isn't the goal (or it wouldn't be failure).

While we don't want to minimize the pain of failure, we do want to give our sons and daughters relief from the fear of it. Fear paralyzes us in exactly the moment that action is called for. Fear slows us down when it's time to go faster—or vice versa. Fear is also evidence that we've diminished our faith in God's absolute strength, love, and goodness and placed our hope elsewhere.

So what exactly are we afraid of when we dread failure? I can think of three things:

1. WE'RE AFRAID OF CONFIRMING OUR INSIGNIFICANCE.

I'm afraid, so to speak, that many of us set our kids up for this brand of fear—in the same way our parents set us up. In our growing-up years, we're most often affirmed for our suc-cesses, and we're affirmed even more loudly for our bigger successes. Over time, an internal message builds that says, "I'm significant because I succeed."

This isn't pop psychology; it just makes sense, right? Why *wouldn't* we praise our kids when they get straight A's, or when they play key roles in winning a big game, or even when they succeed in sitting quietly through a whole church service? Even when we're successfully modeling the truth that we love them unconditionally, we can't help but join the world in say-ing, "What makes you important are your victories."

For certain personalities, especially, this can generate a fear that says, "If I stop succeeding, I'll become insignificant as a person. Failure will prove once and for all that I'm really worthless at my core."

So how can we help our kids (and ourselves) tackle this one—aside from letting them fail well, as we'll talk about later in this chapter? I believe we need to tell them (and ourselves) two very big messages—and do it often.

One: *No matter what our successes, none of us are worth anything on our own without God.*

Two: *No matter how successful we become, we don't become any more significant to God.*

This fear of being proved worthless is really pride in disguise, a belief that I've earned some status as a "worthy person" (which means I can lose it, too). The message of the gospel, however, is that I cannot earn any status with God on my own. I am powerless without God. In fact, I'm God's enemy—doomed for destruction without him. But my worth has been established by the price God paid for me—the life of God's only Son.

That's doctrine. Kids catch on to the attitudes around them. Your attitude toward them in their victories and failures will tell them if you really believe their value is internal—or if it's based on their successes as second basemen or math students or churchgoers. They'll also catch whether or not we're using external measuring sticks of success to prop up our own sense of worth.

2. WE'RE AFRAID OF LOOKING FOOLISH TO OTHERS.

Sometimes you can tell that your kids are driven by fear of failure based on how they behave around new people they like—but whose opinion of them isn't yet clear. At home or with close friends, most kids will just be themselves, whether that's loud and crazy, quiet and focused—or a little of both.

But when a new, desirable personality is introduced, you'll often see a change.

The risk-taking kids might start showing off and performing for the newcomer, hoping to gain approval by getting attention. Kids who are afraid to fail—to be rejected—might become almost inert, unwilling to do or say anything that could make them look foolish.

This seems obvious, but the fear of appearing foolish in our failure—even when it comes to not living up to the unwritten codes of "coolness"—can cripple insecure teenagers as they shift their desire for acceptance from you to their peers.

Adults do the same thing, although we're subtler about it. I'm convinced this is the reason many men who are otherwise confident and secure in their personal lives are afraid to assert themselves in churches. They fear saying or doing something "wrong" that will show they don't know the unwritten codes of being a Christian. They don't want to look like idiots while trying to pray out loud or talk about a Bible they're only just now getting to know.

3. WE DON'T WANT TO WASTE OUR TIME.

Failure can be expensive. In business settings companies can spend millions while attempting new strategies, only to see them fizzle within days of a high-profile launch. At the end of the year, the cost of that failure will be quantified in dollars and attached to the names of those who risked trying it. It's no wonder we're afraid.

But in any setting, failure costs something—whether it's time, money, energy, or emotional investment. You'll see this play out as kids consider what to do with their free time. As you toss out ideas, they might imagine for a second the fun dividend that may or may not result and then decide the effort isn't worth the risk of not enjoying the experience.

For teens battling the inertia of adolescence, this fear of "wasting my time" by doing something that might not deliver on its promise becomes a great deception. It's a lie based on an extremely narrow definition of success. That is, my effort to go out for the track team will only be a success if I make the team and earn medals. Or my effort to get a summer job will only be a success if I, (a) get the job, (b) make enough money, and (c) enjoy the experience.

What we'll see next is that expanding the definition of *success*—and the value of failure—can help address all three of these sources of fear.

Redefining Failure

Some of us have such a stake in our kids' successes that we resist this whole conversation. After all, the great champions just hate to lose, right? It causes them physical pain to drop the ball, to miss the shot, to lose the game in the final seconds. We don't want our kids to get comfortable with failure. We want them to be hungry for victory.

But this brings us back to the core idea of this book. Victory and loss, success and failure are all defined by what story we see ourselves living in. And for those of us who are naturally competitive, this becomes a real test of our faith in God's storyline.

Why? Because the definition of *success* in God's story is 180 degrees away from the definition of *success* in the world's story. For instance, a fair definition of *success* from the world's storyline involves "getting what I want out of life." But James defines *worldly wisdom* as bitter envy and selfish ambition. To put it another way, what it boils down to is "look around and decide what you want" and then "make a plan to go out and get it."

Well, that sounds like pretty good advice from our culture's standpoint, doesn't it? You may have been to seminars that taught you how to do exactly that. But James warns us not to boast about holding on to that worldview. He also warns that the result of living for that version of success is always epic failure in the form of disorder and evil. (See James 3:13-16.)

In God's storyline, however, *success* looks completely different from simply ending up with the life you want. James describes the person who succeeds as living with a life of wisdom: Pure, passionate for peace, thoughtful, submissive, merciful, productive in good things, sincere, and a peacemaker. (See James 3:17-18.) There's no mention of material acquisitions, physical pleasure, or championship rings.

Does that mean it's wrong to succeed in landing pleasure, possessions, and status on our way to winning the big game, being the best in the class, driving the car we've always wanted? No, it's not wrong. For those trying to lead their families along God's storyline, what's wrong is defining any of those things as "success"—or a lack of any of them as "failure."

Here's where the roads divide: God's method of bringing us to his view of success involves experiencing failure. For most of us that's a big counterintuitive idea. So let me say it again in another way: *Our ability to trust God and become more and more like Jesus comes through our experience of loss. And often that includes our failures.*

Let's back up to the very beginning of James to make the point. Remember this? "Consider it pure joy, my brothers, whenever you face trials of many kinds, because you know that the testing of your faith develops perseverance. Perseverance must finish its work so that you may be mature and complete, not lacking anything" (1:2-4).

Failure is one brand of trial. God uses our failures to make us successful as people who trust him. Read those verses again. They don't say, "Consider it joy when trials come, because you know God will make you successful in the end." James tells us to embrace the trials because they lead to trusting God, and trusting God—perseverance in faith—is the definition of success for a Jesus-follower.

It's the gold medal. It's the top rung. Trusting God is the victory.

So when our kids (or when we) face failure—real, painful, want-a-do-over failure—that's the teachable moment, that's the opportunity to show them we're living in God's storyline. We're defining *success*, in that moment, as the ability to continue trusting God even when we fail.

Failing Well in God's Storyline

Most of us miss the opportunity to fail well. Instead of stopping long enough to reinforce our faith in God—not ourselves—in a visible way, we as parents, especially, instinctively rush in to minimize the impact of the failure we fear so acutely. We tell our kids, "It's okay; this failure isn't who you really are. You're still significant. You didn't look too foolish. And it wasn't a waste of your time and energy because you learned a valuable lesson that may make you successful in the world's storyline later."

That last one is a biggie, and it can be very true. Failure can be used to make us more successful later on, which is fine; but that's not the biggest or best use of failure while we're walking in God's storyline. Our point, our hope for our kids, isn't that they simply fail their way to worldly success. We have a different goal.

I believe there are at least six keys to helping our kids benefit from failure from the perspective of God's storyline.

1. RESPOND TO FAILURE WITH HUMILITY.

This sounds obvious, but it's pretty much the opposite of how most of us respond. We're too quick to convince ourselves (and our kids) that failure isn't who we really are.

Yes, it is! Paul encouraged us in Romans to think of ourselves with sober judgment. Let's tell ourselves and our kids the truth "in the inner parts," as David prayed. We're people who sometimes drop the ball. We're people capable of making poor decisions. We're people who willfully sin. We're people who fail tests. And it's not just because the sun was in our eyes, or we stayed up too late, or we weren't feeling well.

We're human beings with definable limits. We fail.

All of us admire people who can laugh at themselves, who can accept their failures as the norm. I love post-game inter-views when the losers acknowledge, "I dropped the ball. I do that sometimes." Notice, though, that this isn't self-flagella-tion. It would be dishonest to then say, "I always drop the ball. I'm a ball-dropper. That's just who I am." Humility means be-ing honest about *catching* the ball, too. Or passing the test. Or winning the championship.

Either way, the key to humility is that neither we nor our kids define ourselves according to what we accomplish. We define ourselves—and our success—by who God is.

2. BE HONEST ABOUT THE PAIN AND FRUSTRATION.

Refusing to define ourselves by it might diminish the pain of failure, but it still hurts. We should be able to admit that. Some of us, maybe especially tweens, can be overly positive about failure, pretending they aren't disappointed.

This fear of admitting that we care comes from our need to protect our sense of self-worth, our pride. But the productive work of failure is found in the pain that comes with it. If we deny or gloss over the pain, we rob failure of the good it can bring us.

It's the pain that drives us to put our hope more deeply in our Father. The sense of loss motivates us to fill up the emptiness of chasing the world's self-glorifying storyline with the fullness of the hope built into God's God-glorifying one.

3. BE HONEST ABOUT WHAT WENT WRONG.

With the pain of the failure in one hand and humility in the other, we're ready to do a little analysis and figure out what went wrong. *Did we stay up too late? Did we make some false assumptions? Were we overconfident in our commitments? Did we fail to act in God's power? Did we play to our weaknesses instead of our strengths?*

Again, though, the point of this exercise isn't that we'll become better people if we fail less frequently. The point is learning to walk in practical wisdom for God's glory. And it's a profound teaching point to use failures as a way of eliminating bad choices the next time.

As good ol' Thomas Edison is said to have uttered—breaking Keys 1 and 2 but following Key 3—"I have not failed. I've just found 10,000 ways that won't work."

4. LOOK FOR GOD'S DIRECTION IN THE FAILURE.

Nearly everyone I know can point to the great failures in their lives as being the stepping-stones God used to put them in the positions God meant for them all along. Have you told your kids your stories about those direction-changing failures in your own life?

I know several men who poured all of their resources into building a business. They schemed, prayed, planned, and executed—and it all collapsed anyway. With all of their resources gone, they were forced to trust God in a way they'd never imagined and then watch as God led each of them to even better-fitting jobs or businesses than the one they'd all hoped for.

If they could've seen the future, they would've known that the dreams they so passionately worked for were too small. Failure was the path God used to bring them to better dreams for his glory.

It sometimes works that way in relationships as well. A good friend of mine tells the story of a girl who was "just perfect" for him in "nearly every way." And she liked him, too. But he failed in the relationship. He didn't treat her well. He was immature. He blew it, driving her away. But that failure allowed time for him to grow in the grace of God and, practically, it meant he was available (and more mature) when his eventual wife and lifelong best friend came along.

If his dreams of a life with the first woman had come true—if he hadn't blown it—he wouldn't have been in the place God needed him to be to meet his wife.

These stories aren't meant as false salves to make us feel okay about honest failure. They're meant to make us see this next point more clearly.

5. REMEMBER HOW MUCH BIGGER GOD IS THAN OUR FAILURES.

This is the biggest message I want my kids to hear about failure. They're too small and too insignificant to put a dent in God's plan for the universe. And, often, they're even too small to put a dent in God's plan for their own lives!

What we're talking about here is a radical faith—living and walking in God's storyline. It's the same faith Joseph carried in his wounded heart. Joseph's brothers failed enormously. They failed willfully. They failed morally. They sold their brother to slave traders. They lied to their dad, who loved Joseph deeply, and said Joseph was dead. That's an epic failure.

You know the story. Joseph ends up as the second most powerful man in the world and in the perfect position—many, many painful years later—to save his family from starvation and ruin. By faith he believed his brothers' failure was also God's great plan. Remember these words? "You intended to harm me, but God intended it for good to accomplish what is now being done, the saving of many lives" (Genesis 50:20).

The point of this isn't that we should sin with abandon since God will work out his plan anyway. Rather, our choices still have consequences, as we saw in the previous chapter. Joseph suffered as a result of his brothers' actions. Our decisions matter, and our failures are our own.

But—and this is a giant interjection—God is far, far more powerful than the impact of our failures. Trying something new, taking a risk, going for the home-run swing—nothing we attempt is going to throw God off the path of his own storyline.

6. TRY SOMETHING RISKIER.

Our last point about responding to failure is this: When your kids fail, urge them to try again and try something riskier. Again, this is counterintuitive. Our instinct is to pull back, to play it safe, to hide. Our fear of failure in the face of failure expands. Maybe it even begins to control us.

One way to overcome timidity in the face of small failures is to dare ourselves and our kids to risk bigger ones. There's no better way to say, "My self-image and how others think of me isn't the most important thing. My time and energy and money aren't the most important things. I won't be the prisoner of my fear of failure. I'll try something even riskier."

Now, obviously, wisdom limits the kinds of risky things we're talking about. We're not looking for risky moral compromises or foolish actions that involve borrowing large sums of money or being unkind to people or feeding our own ego or engaging in physically dangerous stunts. What we're talking about is risking another failure to accomplish something worthwhile that might be at the edge of our imagined capabilities. We're talking about putting our inner selves so far out there that we don't know for sure if we'll fly or fall.

In addition to being a brave response to failure, this approach also forces us to trust God in endeavors bigger than our individual abilities can handle. It forces us to say, "God can handle this, no matter how it turns out. If I jump and miss, God's able to set me down anywhere he wishes. I'm willing to lose—or succeed—in my attempt because I know God is the one who'll keep me walking in his storyline."

Helping your kids make these kinds of scary attempts while they're still young is a gift. But even so, are you truly convinced God is at work in our successes and our failures?

That sometimes our failures even fit into his plan for the universe—and for our ultimate success as people who trust him completely?

Don't be afraid to fail in front of your kids. *But do be concerned about failing to fail well in front of them.* And do be concerned if your kids seem overly afraid of failing. It might be just the thing they need in order to see Christ as their Savior and themselves as his servants—instead of the other way around.

Before you move on to the next chapter, ask yourself these questions:

1. Have you ever sensed that your kids are afraid to fail? If so, how much of that fear comes from their own personalities as opposed to the emphasis on success and failure in your home?

2. What are a few of your most productive failures? How did they help you to grow as a person and/or as a follower of Jesus? Does your family know about those failures and your attitude toward them now?

3. What do you believe could be your child's next opportunity to fail in something that matters to him or her? How can you begin to prepare your child to see honest failure in that area as an opportunity to walk successfully in God's storyline?

Chapter Nine

SO MANY STORIES: SEEING ENTERTAINMENT THROUGH THE LENS OF GOD'S STORY

We've spent much of this book talking about seeing a Christian and biblical worldview as God's story, his version—the true version—of how the universe operates, of who the key players are, of what the central conflict in life is, and where victory over that conflict comes from. God's Word provides us with a beginning, middle, and ending to the story of all things. Part of what we do as parents is help our kids see how our little stories fit into God's big story.

So Many Stories: Seeing Entertainment through the Lens of God's Story

This language resonates with us because we're all conditioned to consume information as stories. We hear, watch, read, and listen to thousands of stories every year. Some of them are factual: The best news stories are structured to introduce us to casts of real-life characters—and the stories have beginnings, middles, and endings—even if the complete stories aren't yet known. Similarly, each sporting event is a natural story, complete with colorful characters, an obvious central conflict, and a satisfying resolution (at least for the winners). And we tell each other the continuing stories of our personal days and lives, sometimes in bite-size morsels of 140 characters or less.

But most of the stories we mentally ingest are fictional. They come in the form of novels, TV shows, movies, three-minute pop songs, and video games. And each one of those stories is built on a given set of assumptions about how the world works. Each story has a perspective on life. We recognize that as the story's worldview.

For instance, a detective novel in which the murder victim has been killed for his life insurance money is, at the very least, built on the worldview that some people care more about money than they do about human life. If the novel suggests that person should be apprehended and locked up, it's built on a worldview in which morality exists and justice is embraced. The story is told from the point of view that right and wrong are real things, at least to some extent.

Another example might come in the form of a sweeping love story between a man and a woman who overcome great obstacles before they finally end up together in a committed relationship. Such a story reveals to us that the storyteller's worldview includes romantic love as a valuable and desirable connection between two people. If the couple has sex without hesitation or consequence before getting married, that would tell us something about the storyteller's perspective on that area of life.

So why are we talking about this? Because story is a powerful teacher, especially for kids. Every story teaches something, even if the storyteller's main intent is simply to entertain. And most stories carry at least one or two overt messages as well.

All of these stories present us parents with powerful teaching opportunities. If we're willing to make the effort to dive into some of these stories with our children, we'll discover worldviews that both confirm and deny God's view of life. And those truths and lies can become equally effective means of helping youth examine their own biblically based worldviews.

Most parents are used to thinking about protecting their children from various media content. To varying degrees, we're on the lookout for graphic violence, sexual situations, harsh language, and adult themes in the TV shows, music, books, and Internet content our kids consume. Depending on the age of our kids, that watchdog status can definitely become a burden.

On the other hand, I rarely find parents as eager to evaluate media based on the worldview messages they contain, even when those messages so clearly and persuasively stand in direct opposition to God's story, which we're trying to share with our kids.

Several years ago, we started noticing at Planet Wisdom how Christian teens often seemed to endorse the false messages of the movies and TV shows they loved while maintaining their firm conviction in the truthfulness of the Word of God. They didn't seem to understand that these opposing ideas couldn't be true simultaneously.

So Many Stories: Seeing Entertainment through the Lens of God's Story

For instance, a well-made 1999 film called *The Cider House Rules*, based on a book by John Irving, tells the story of a young man named Homer Wells (played by the likable actor Tobey Maguire) who learns important life lessons in the 1940s while becoming a compassionate doctor who cares for migrant farm workers.

However, the lessons Homer learns come from his drug-addicted mentor (played by the likable Michael Caine) and from sleeping with the girlfriend of a World War II bomber pilot behind the man's back. And one of those lessons includes learning to accept the role of becoming a doctor who performs illegal abortions for needy women.

The film is gorgeous to watch, shot in the golden hues of autumn and carried along by a romantic and beautiful score. It's emotional and moving. And late in the story its central message is delivered by that respected older doctor who talks about breaking the rules of law and morality: "The people who made those rules don't live here. They don't breathe this air. They don't spend their time here. Those rules aren't for us. We make our own rules, don't we, Homer?"

Unless you've seen the film, you'll have to take my word for it. But that statement being delivered by that character at that moment in the film comes across as deeply wise and insightful and brave. And yet it's exactly the opposite of the truth. Whatever one's stance on the divisive issue of abortion rights, that statement describing the world's best wisdom runs in direct opposition to the wisdom of God.

My hope for parents is not simply to discover what kinds of ideas are taught in movies and forbid their kids from seeing those kinds of films. Instead I hope we can help our kids whenever they encounter these stories to view them through the wisdom of God and say, "That's not true from my under-standing of what the Bible teaches...and here's why."

On the positive side, another movie starring Tobey Magu-ire was the box-office dominating *Spider-Man* (2002). The loudest message of that particular film is one that easily fits into the framework of God's larger story: "With great power comes great responsibility." I'd love teens to explain what that means within the context of the film, as well as to explain why it's true within the context of the Word of God.

Is that too much to expect? I don't think so, but it does take some specific training. And how we as parents model the consumption of entertainment will have a lot to do with whether or not our kids ever get around to making that ef-fort. If we insist, "It's just entertainment," then we won't help them process all the stories they'll hear over the course of their lives, many of which have yet to be told and by a variety of storytellers from every possible worldview perspective.

God's story of the Christian life doesn't seem to leave room for the modern view of "entertainment," letting story after story wash over us without ever engaging our minds in evaluating truth and error. Instead God calls us to "take cap-tive every thought" (2 Corinthians 10:5), to dwell on "what-ever is true...whatever is lovely" (Philippians 4:8), and to set aside the world's wisdom in favor of God's. I don't believe we can do that if we don't listen to every story with a critical ear for truth and falsehood.

We'll model how to do that at the end of this chapter. For now, let's tackle a more obvious question for most of us who worry about what our kids are feeding their souls from the entertainment troughs of the world: *How can we teach them how to decide what's worth taking in and what isn't?*

Should I Watch This?

For now—and depending on the age of your son(s) or daughter(s)—you might still be in the position of saying yes or no to what media your child is allowed to watch or listen to or what video games to play. Inevitably, though, those decisions will be theirs and theirs alone. How will they decide what to take in when you're not the final word on those choices? Or, if they're already making most of those decisions themselves, how are they deciding now?

Part of their decision-making process will be built on the choices they've seen you make. Of course, most teens will begin to push your limits a step further. That's the nature of adolescence. But they'll have picked up some cues from you about how to establish limits—or *if* they should establish them.

The following self-evaluation questions are good tools for kids and adults alike to use when making choices about whether to say yes or no to various media options. Before we get to them, though, I should share what I've noticed about some parents of the Christian teens I spend time with: They're a lot like me!

By that I mean they're almost as eager as their kids are to talk about movies, TV shows, and the latest video games. And we're all a little protective of our "right" to watch whatever we want to watch. We're the grown-ups, after all. And we'd rather not have to deal with anyone—especially other Christians—trying to set standards for us. Those uptight restrictions should have gone away with our parents' generation, right?

Well, yes—to a point. But I'd also say that one benefit of being a parent is the opportunity to look at yourself as a child again—because being parents makes us question who we are and how we're growing. So ask yourself some questions as well: *What attitudes do I hope my kids will bring into a conversation about their media choices? With what kind of spirit do I hope they'll approach this topic as they move on into their adulthood? Does what they watch, hear, and play impact them on a spiritual, emotional, and mental level?* I believe it's safe to say it does.

As I model for my kids what it means to walk in God's story in an age of millions of media choices and too little time to consume everything, I should be willing to ask myself those same questions. *What attitude will I bring to the issue of my media choices? Does what I watch, hear, and play impact me on a spiritual, emotional, and mental level?*

Because our media choices are nearly unlimited, and because our media consumption can be nearly anonymous, I believe it's important to be willing to approach this conversation with ourselves and with our kids with three specific attitudes:

1. A Submissive Spirit

When it comes to media, are we—or are our kids—here to "fight for our right to par-take?" (That's a little Beastie Boys play on words for you old-timers.) Or are we wiling to surrender something as minor as a half-hour of *Two and a Half Men* if we become convinced that's what God wants from us?

2. A Ruthless Self-Honesty

David wrote that God wants us to have truth in the inner parts. Have you ever noticed your kids trying to talk themselves into or out of feeling a certain way about the media they're taking in? "No, Daddy. I'm not scared," they might say while hiding their eyes from the screen. Have you ever tried to talk yourself into believing that some media experience doesn't feel unhealthy to you?

3. A Sensitivity to the Holy Spirit

Some of us—and some of our children—can work up a good guilt about almost anything. That's not what we're talking about. Our desire for ourselves and for our kids is learning to let the Holy Spirit nudge (or shove) our spirits in the direction of making good media choices. But that takes a willingness to listen to God.

Okay, now we're ready to look at some of the questions we use at Planet Wisdom to train our children to take responsibility for asking and answering when it comes to their media choices.

1. Have I had enough already? The issue isn't always the quality of or the objectionable content in our media. There's so much of every kind of story out there now that you could watch, play, listen, or read eight hours a day for the rest of your life and never run out. We all know there's such a thing as too much, but the media machine is built to keep feeding us the next bite.

I won't bother to regurgitate the studies showing the links between TV watching and performance in school or creativity or attention span or obesity. You've read them. And they mostly make us feel bad anytime anyone in the family sits down to watch the television.

However, for our purposes as Real World Parents, we should recognize the power of having our kids see us saying "enough" to ourselves and not just to them. There's a value in sharing with them our thought process for disconnecting from entertainment or anything else in our lives, to model for them how we arrive at moderation in our media consumption.

Moderation is a tricky word. It's easier, after all, to put absolute limits on media consumption ("You may watch/listen/read for one hour. Period."). And it's also easier to just give up and let them saturate themselves to their levels of interest. To model and teach where the line is between "enough" and "too much" takes more time and effort. But it pays off in kids who begin to ask the question, "Do I even want to keep doing this? How will it help me with anything? Could I do something more fun or interesting with my time?"

2. Have my parents said no? I spent several years as a media advice columnist for *Ignite Your Faith* (formerly *Campus Life*) magazine. As a parent you may (or may not, I guess) be surprised by how many teens wrote to me looking for a second opinion. "Dear Dr. Matlock: My parents have diagnosed the Harry Potter books as inappropriate for me at this point in my development. I'm wondering if I should read them anyway and if you think there's anything wrong with them?"

I don't know why, but some kids suffer disconnects between their media choices and submission to parental authority. In a Bible quiz, they'd absolutely answer correctly that children should obey their parents. But then they quickly dismiss what their parents tell them later that night regarding what they're reading/watching/playing.

Obviously, we can command, and we can discipline for such disobedience. But there's also room for having a conversation about how walking in God's story means being men and women under authority, too. It's worth sharing your own struggles to submit to the authorities God has placed in your life and to believe that God directs your circumstances through the restrictions and directions of those in charge—even when they're wrong.

It's a hard thing for kids to believe that what goes into their brains really matters. And it's a hard thing for all of us to believe that God might be directing our steps through the authorities in our lives. But those are lessons we hope our kids will at least wrestle with, even if they don't always find the will to act on faith.

Remember, the eventual goal is to raise kids who make wise media choices on their own, not because you "said so." Wise parents begin to loosen the reins on what's allowed as their kids get older. I've admired friends of mine who've given their children permission to take in things that might have been restricted a year or two earlier with the caveat that their kids would either write a report or have a conversation about the story based on some of the worldview analysis we'll describe in the next few pages.

3. Will consuming this media make it easier for me to sin or do good? Notice that this is a step back from the absolutist question that may have been asked when we were kids: "Is it a sin for me to watch or listen to or play this?" Scripture lowers the bar but raises the stakes on media choices when Paul quotes an early motto among believers no longer under the weight of the law—"Everything is permissible"—and then quickly follows it with "but not everything is beneficial" and "but not everything is constructive." (See 1 Corinthians 10:23.)

We're trying to teach our families to ask harder questions than just, "Is it okay to watch such-and-such movie?" or "Is it okay to listen to such-and-such band?" If you want to drive them crazy, ask back, "Will watching that movie be beneficial?" or "Will listening to that band be constructive?"

And if you want them to believe that *you believe* those are valid questions, then practice applying them to what you watch and hear and read. It's actually a really hard question. An easier way to put it might be, "Will this thing make me more or less likely to sin, more or less likely to do good?" Because, really, there's very little that we take in that leaves us absolutely neutral in our responding desires.

4. Will this media choice make me struggle with fear? There's a kind of fear you experience when your kids hide around the corner and then jump out and scare you. Some media is packed with those kinds of "jump in your seat" moments. And then there's the kind of fear that lingers in your mind with each dreaded step toward the darkness and shadows of your silent bedroom. Any parent who's spent a sleepless night with a freaked-out kid understands that fear all too well.

Here's one thing we know for sure: God doesn't want us to live in fear. It's one of the most often delivered commands in the New Testament. God empowers those walking in his story to overcome fear. To choose to hold on to it for the sake of entertainment would be a shame.

But it takes some kids a while to figure out where their lines are between enjoying the "scary parts" of a movie or book and being owned by the scary parts long after they've finished the stories. We're not all the same, and your kids might have very different tolerance levels than you have. But encourage them not to sacrifice peace of mind for the sake of any story.

5. Will this media choice make me struggle with sexually inappropriate, confusing, or immoral thoughts? Clearly, this is a question for kids to ask as they get older. Once you've decided to have "the talk" and opened the door to discussing issues of sexuality with your sons or daughters, it's entirely appropriate to include media choices in the conversation. For now, most parents see it as part of their mandate to stand between their kids' eyeballs and the kind of sexual content so readily available online, on TV, in music, in books, at friends' houses, on random commercials, in random magazines and catalogs, in conversations in your driveway with neighbor kids...

Okay, so you're going to have a hard time standing between your kids and every possible source of sexually charged storytelling. It's more than appropriate—in fact, it's entirely necessary—to find ways to have open dialogue with kids about why what they see in the media stories is often so very different from God's plan for sex as you've described it to them.

An even bigger deal is maintaining an approachable spirit or not freaking out when the day comes that they get an eyeful of content you wish they'd never seen—or when you find out they've been feeding themselves content you didn't even know existed. What we do and say in those moments matters because it tells them how confident we are in God's mercy, grace, patience, and forgiveness. What we do and say also tells them how seriously we take God's standards for sexuality.

Finally, the choices that our kids see us making about sexual content in our own entertainment choices communicate volumes to them as well.

It's a valid question for us to ask our sons (and vice versa) to wrestle with being like Job—who pledged never to look lustfully at a woman (Job 31:1)—while living with a TV set that seems to have been built for that very purpose. What lines will they draw for themselves after they leave your house (or enter their bedrooms) to make that possible?

6. Will this media choice make me struggle with anger? I will quote this study to you because it confirms what a lot of research about teens and video games has been suggesting for a while.

For a 2006 study conducted by the Indiana University School of Medicine, researchers hooked up 44 adolescents to MRI machines that map brain activity. Then they had the students play fast-paced video games, with half the group playing violent games and the other half playing nonviolent games.

The results clearly showed that those who played the violent games had significantly different responses in two parts of their brains. First, they experienced more activity in a region associated with "emotional arousal." In other words, they got seriously hyped up. And second, they experienced less activity in a brain region associated with self-control. As a result, violent video game players tended to be more worked up and less inhibited than other players.[14]

I'm not saying that means no kids should ever play video games with violence—or video games at all. I love video games, and my family has enjoyed playing some fantastic games together, often leaving us pretty hyped up. Gaming is here to stay, and it's become a new norm in family entertainment and togetherness.

What we do know for sure, though, is that God's will is for us not to hold on to anger—any kind of anger. If playing particular games or listening to certain music leaves us angry and with lower inhibitions, then that's a problem. Paul's list of flavors of anger in Colossians 3:8 is comprehensive, and he tells us to get rid of all of it: "But now you must rid yourselves of all such things as these: anger, rage, malice, slander, and filthy language from your lips."

If we (or our kids) get sinfully angry during or after consuming any particular kind of media, then it's probably not God's will for us (or them) to participate in it any longer. I've

---

14. http://www.medicine.indiana.edu/news_releases/archive_02/violent_games02.html

had Christian friends tell me straight up that they like certain kinds of hard rock music because it helps them stay angry and energized. I don't believe that's God's will for them. Others I know are able to plug into Metallica for hours at a time without any noticeable rage rising to the surface.

Similarly, if any media creates discord, anger, and tension in your home, grab the opportunity to explain to your kids why you're choosing to limit their exposure to it. Even if they angrily disagree with your choice, they should at least be able to understand that you're honestly trying to lead your family to walk in God's storyline by your response to anger-making media.

Can They Say What the Story Is Saying?

Now that we've dealt with some of the questions related to how beneficial particular media is, we come to what I believe is an even better question: *When I watch or play or listen to or read a news story, can I spot the worldview the story is built on? Can I hear and describe the messages that story is delivering? And, most importantly, can I compare the story's worldview to a biblical perspective?*

We already described at the beginning of this chapter why worldview analysis matters. It's a cause we've been championing in the area of movies at PlanetWisdom.com for nearly a decade. In each review, we break down a synopsis of the story, give a quick opinion of what our reviewer thought about the movie on its own terms, and then dive into the exercise described here.

We try to say as clearly and fairly as possible what the movie is saying about the nature of life, of good and evil, of human nature, of the reality of God, and so on. And then we try to show how that perspective compares to what God's story tells us about those things.

If, as Real World Parents, we hope to keep ourselves and our kids from becoming victims of the thousands of mixed messages in our media—and if we hope to give them (and us) some means of redeeming the hours spent consuming all that media—I believe we must own the responsibility to teach our kids these skills.

What we're hoping for is raising Christian thinkers, not just Christian consumers. Anytime I hear teens say something like, "I know I shouldn't watch it, but it was a great movie," that tells me that (a) they're only processing media in terms of "should or shouldn't," not in terms of "What did it say?" and (b) "should or shouldn't" doesn't really matter to them any-way. If they—and most of the rest of us—are going to truly leave behind the ineffective "should or shouldn't" of mindless legalism, then we must also be able to carefully think about what we're participating in.

Another statement I hear a lot from kids—and this is a step in the right direction—is, "I don't agree with some of the stuff in it, but I liked the story." We'd like to hear kids take one more step forward and say, from a biblical point of view, what they didn't agree with in the storyteller's per-spective and why—without apologizing, necessarily, for en-joying the storytelling.

How do we get them there? We've put together the fol-lowing list of questions that can be asked in regard to just about any story in any format, whether song or game or mov-ie or book. A great place to start would be to take in some kind of story with your family, then work through the follow-ing questions as an exercise in building biblical discernment about what our media is telling us.

Story Worldview Analysis

1. WHAT DOES THE STORY SAY ABOUT GOD?

Most secular stories seem to exist in a world in which God doesn't meaningfully exist. Some create a version of God that's different than what Scripture shows. Some, though, leave room for the possibility of God's existence or even come right out and make the case for a biblically compatible version of the Creator.

2. WHAT DOES THE STORY SAY ABOUT JESUS?

Any story that suggests humans can have peace with God without a relationship with Jesus are misrepresenting God's story. Does this one mention Jesus in any meaningful way? If so, what does it say about him?

3. WHAT DOES THE STORY SAY ABOUT THE SUPERNATURAL WORLD?

Are other gods or religions presented as valid and positive? Are angels or demons mentioned? Ghosts? How do the story's descriptions of those things line up with the Bible's teaching?

4. WHAT DOES THE STORY SAY ABOUT GOOD AND EVIL OR RIGHT AND WRONG?

Within the worldview of the story, are some things assumed to be right and others wrong? Do the characters desire and work for justice when wrong is done? Is evil shown as being truly evil? Does good exist?

5. WHAT DOES THE STORY SAY ABOUT THE NATURE OF HUMAN BEINGS?

Are human beings seen as all good, some good and some bad, or all bad? Are humans assumed to be improving morally as a species, or on the decline?

6. WHAT DOES THE STORY SAY ABOUT GRACE AND REDEMPTION?

Are human beings shown to be entirely self-sufficient, or in need of grace and forgiveness? Can people within this world redeem themselves, or do they need a savior of some kind?

7. WHAT DOES THE STORY SAY ABOUT PARENTS AND FAMILIES?

8. WHAT DOES THE STORY SAY ABOUT SEX AND MARRIAGE?

9. WHAT DOES THE STORY SAY ABOUT REVENGE AND JUSTICE?

10. WHAT THE STORY SAY ABOUT TRUTH AND LYING?

11. WHAT IN THIS STORY ESPECIALLY DISAGREES WITH GOD'S STORY OF THE UNIVERSE?

12. WHAT IN THIS STORY ESPECIALLY AGREES WITH GOD'S STORY?

13. WHAT CAN WE LEARN ABOUT LIFE FROM THIS STORYTELLER'S UNIQUE POINT OF VIEW?

14. WHAT DID WE AGREE OR DISAGREE WITH REGARDING THIS STORY'S WORLDVIEW JUST BECAUSE THAT'S OUR OPINION—AND NOT DUE TO AN ISSUE OF BIBLICAL TRUTH?

As you begin to walk with your children through questions like these, it will begin to sink in. Over time it will become second nature to listen to our stories through the filter of God's story, to evaluate each story's messages in terms of truthfulness and error. You and your family can begin to move past "should or shouldn't" to sorting out the false wisdom from the godly wisdom on display in books, games, TV shows, music, and movies.

Another helpful thing about learning to listen to stories from God's perspective is that we become better storytellers ourselves. And as we'll see in the next chapter, we don't want to forget to tell our kids the exciting conclusion to the biggest story of all.

Before you move on to the next chapter, ask yourself these questions:

1. How often do you evaluate the entertainment stories you and your family take in every day (in terms of their truthfulness in regard to God's storyline)?

2. How many stories can you and your children meaningfully evaluate in a single day or week? Should that limit the number of stories (shows, video games, books, movies, etc.) you all digest?

Chapter Ten

TELLING THE END OF THE STORY

I remember a dark moment in my freshman year of college. I was confused about a romantic relationship. I wasn't sure why I was in school. I'd lost sight of who I was, in a way, and felt like I was in trouble. I called my dad for help. It was one o'clock in the morning.

Dad didn't get mad. He didn't dismiss my feelings as that of a stressed-out college kid. He took me seriously and asked if I'd like to talk about it in person. And then he got in his car, in the middle of the night, and drove out to meet me. And what I took away from that conversation was more than just a renewed realization of how much my dad cared about me. He also helped me to get my hope back in the right place. He helped me see that I'd been looking for hope in a relationship with a girl and in going to college, and those hopes had failed.

Dad helped me put my hope back in God.

There's that great speech at the end of *The Two Towers*, in the Lord of the Rings trilogy, where Frodo's faithful servant and companion, Sam, realizes they're at the low point in the adventure where everything's going wrong. Sam says:

> "It's like in the great stories, Mr. Frodo. The ones that really mattered. Full of darkness and danger they were. And sometimes you didn't want to know the end. Because how could the end be happy? How could the world go back to the way it was when so much bad had happened? Those were the stories that stayed with you. That meant something. Even if you were too small to understand why... Folk in those stories had lots of chances of turning back, only they didn't. Because they were holding on to something...There's some good in this world, Mr. Frodo. And it's worth fighting for."

Telling the End of the Story

No matter how hard we try to protect them, no matter how well we prepare them, our sons and daughters will come to those devastating moments of darkness and danger when they say, as Frodo did, "I can't do this, Sam." Whether or not they continue on will have a lot to do with where their hope is, what they believe to be waiting at the end of the story, what they believe to be the payoff of enduring the great adventure.

In Proverbs 13:12, we're told, "Hope deferred makes the heart sick." Many families—even Christian families—are heartsick today because they've slipped into the world's storyline of believing there's hope in something the world has to offer. Money. Status. Pleasure. Academic achievement. Professional success. Sex. A house. A car. A gadget. A party. A spouse. A baby.

They (we) keep chasing—and even catching—some of these things, but the payoff is always brief and the letdown lingers. And then it's off to the races again after a new false hope. "I'd finally be happy if only..."

The book of Ecclesiastes starts out as a kind of test of all the most popular "if onlys" in the world to see if any of them bring any real meaning to life. Would any of them be enough to become the "good in the world" that Sam so poignantly describes as "worth fighting for"?

I'm convinced that Ecclesiastes is Solomon's creation. As the wisest and richest of all men, he was uniquely qualified to conduct this test. He had unlimited wealth and power with which to gain access to all of the "if onlys," but he also had deep access to the wisdom of God to test the results for meaning and purpose. His conclusion was that nothing "under the sun" was meaningful.

Read what he writes in chapter two, verses 4 through 11.

> I undertook great projects: I built houses for myself and planted vineyards. I made gardens and parks and planted all kinds of fruit trees in them. I made reservoirs to water groves of flourishing trees. I bought male and female slaves and had other slaves who were born in my house. I also owned more herds and flocks than anyone in Jerusalem before me. I amassed silver and gold for myself, and the treasure of kings and provinces. I acquired

men and women singers, and a harem as well—
the delights of the heart of man. I became greater
by far than anyone in Jerusalem before me. In all
this my wisdom stayed with me.

I denied myself nothing my eyes desired; I refused
my heart no pleasure. My heart took delight in all
my work, and this was the reward for all my labor.

Yet when I surveyed all that my hands had done
and what I had toiled to achieve, everything was
meaningless, a chasing after the wind; nothing was
gained under the sun.

Solomon did it all. He experienced epic romance (see Song
of Songs) and epic sexual conquest with nearly 1,000 wives
and concubines. He experienced great industrial achievement
and created undeniable works of art. His wealth and power
allowed him to refuse his heart no pleasure.

And still, he could find nothing in any of it to make the
end of the story worth fighting for. And that will ever and always be the case for those living in the world's storyline and
limiting their search for happy endings to lives lived apart
from the God of the universe.

Hope in the Darkness

If our children see us in a heartsick chase for false hopes,
they may very well join us on that path. But if they see us
stubbornly confronting the inevitable darkness of this life by
clinging to our hope in God, they may echo David's words
from Psalm 43:5—"Why are you downcast, O my soul? Why
so disturbed within me? Put your hope in God, for I will yet
praise him, my Savior and my God."

When they look at our approach to life, what will our children find to help them lift up their downcast souls? Our challenge is to be convinced of God's storyline—beginning, middle, and ending—to the point that our hope in him is unmistakable. And then keep telling our kids the end of the story.

As Augustine put it, "Thou hast made us for Thyself, O God, and our hearts are restless until we find our rest in Thee."

We must be careful, as the church and as families, not to communicate to each other a false hope even within God's storyline. Too many teens, I believe, catch the idea that being in Christ means avoiding real pain in the world, avoiding tragedy, avoiding dark days. We somehow communicate to them that Jesus is a means toward happy circumstances in the world instead of the truth that Jesus is the means to a happily-ever-after in his kingdom.

Then, when painful reality descends, those living in that false hope are tempted to cast Jesus aside as just another failed promise, one he never made in the first place. In fact, Jesus warns us of life's difficulties, even as he stands by us: "In this world you will have trouble. But take heart! I have overcome the world" (John 16:33).

So what does Jesus promise us through faith in him? He promises what Solomon could never have because he conducted his test "under the sun" and before the death and resurrection of the Son. He promises us what Sam vaguely referenced as "some good thing" in the world. He promises us that our faithful service in the darkest parts of the story will mean something and that the story will end in triumph, with the heroes joyous and the villains vanquished forever.

Jesus doesn't promise to end our earthly suffering. But he promises that something far greater than simple comforts will emerge from the suffering of those who are in Christ Jesus: "We also rejoice in our sufferings, because we know that suffering produces perseverance; perseverance, character; and character, hope. And hope does not disappoint us" (Romans 5:3-5).

What we must demonstrate for our kids is that God did not save us to make our lives better; God created and saved us to tell his story. Listen to the prophet Isaiah as he quotes God's voice: "Bring my sons from afar and my daughters from the ends of the earth—everyone who is called by my name, whom I created for my glory, whom I formed and made" (43:6-7).

We aren't just living in God's story; we're part of what's being told. We exist to be used by God in the telling of it forever. That's our great purpose and that is the great hope that brings us meaning—even when the dim hopes of the world look so attractive to us.

The Call to Adventure

Have you ever noticed that in most of the great stories, the hero starts out as the "reluctant hero"? That's Storytelling 101. It's part of what's famously known as the Hero's Journey.

Remember *Star Wars*? Han Solo agrees to help Obi-Wan and Luke and Leia—but only for a price. He's a businessman. He serves himself. He goes on the adventure, sure, but he does so following the world's storyline question of "What's in it for me?" At some point in the Hero's Journey, though, the hero always makes the choice to jump in all the way. For Han Solo, that moment comes at the end of the film (in the original, *Episode 4*) when he comes back to help Luke blow up the Death Star, at great risk to himself, even though he's already been paid.

As Christians all of us make decisions about how much of ourselves we're willing to give to serving God's Story, even at the cost of our own comfort, wealth, security, or pleasure. We all start out as "reluctant heroes." And at some point, many of us choose to begin sacrificing ourselves in service to God as disciples of Jesus. We agree to take up our crosses and follow him by losing our lives to find the part of God's story that he's written for us.

Here are a few hard questions for many parents—even for those who've sacrificed greatly to serve God: *Are you hopeful that your children will answer Christ's call to adventure? Are you willing to see them sacrifice their lives in pursuit of God's glory, as they're called to do, even if it means they don't end up in safe, secure places with happy, friendly people and a good retirement plan? Even if your grandchildren end up poor and living far away?*

In other words, *What parts of God's story are you communicating that you hope they'll play?*

My parents faced this question when my younger twin brothers were in the eighth grade and invited on a dangerous mission trip into the Soviet Union. I know for a fact many parents wouldn't have allowed it, citing safety concerns (and reasonably so).

But Mom and Dad demonstrated profound confidence in God's protection and provision during that trip. They wholeheartedly believed my brothers belonged to God and that God wanted to use them for his glory. And their Real World choices backed that up. As I mentioned in the first chapter, one of those brothers is a senior pastor in a church today; the other one is serving as a missionary in Moscow.

Not all Christian parents are so convinced that God's storyline is the only one worth following. Over the course of my dating career, the parents of the girls I liked always seemed to like me as well. I was a nice guy, after all. Clean-cut. Christian. Good family. What's not to like? But when those parents learned I was planning to enter the foreign mission field, they suddenly treated me like I had the swine flu. They didn't like the idea of *their* beloved daughters swabbing sores in some mud hut in Africa.

God didn't call me to foreign missions, but I know my parents would've fully supported that decision if he did. How about your kids? Will they have your full blessing to follow God's leading in their lives anywhere in the world? That blessing from you, that support, might mean the difference between a lifetime of dangerous-yet-fulfilling adventure and a life of complacent prosperity that looks a lot like the world's story.

One of our greatest—and, honestly, most difficult—tasks is to allow God's will to take hold in our children, including when it doesn't go hand-in-hand with our own "will" for them. Most of us experience varying degrees of tension between the two, but we must read the story again and convince ourselves that their best lives are found by answering God's call.

Hearing the Story, Accepting the Call

If you're pulling for your kids to respond to God's story in the most active way possible, there's only one response that makes sense, only one logical conclusion for what we (or they) should do with our lives when we understand what God's story is all about.

And, of course, it's all about God. It's God's story, and God has—by his otherworldly, indescribable mercy—included us in the story as the "good guys," on the side of the one true King. Not content to leave us lost in our sin in the kingdom of darkness, God sent his Son to die for our sins, to rescue us, and to bring us back as God's children into the Kingdom of Light.

Paul's doxology in Romans 11:33-36 clearly describes how fully this story is God's alone and how deeply unearned our part in any of it must be:

> Oh, the depth of the riches of the wisdom and
> knowledge of God!
>
> How unsearchable his judgments,
>
> and his paths beyond tracing out!
>
> "Who has known the mind of the Lord?
>
> Or who has been his counselor?"
>
> "Who has ever given to God,
>
> that God should repay him?"
>
> For from him and through him and to him
> are all things.
>
> To him be the glory forever! Amen.

How can we ever respond to that? Why would we ever ask, "What's in it for me?" Why would we ever see the privilege of walking in God's story as second best to anything? What's the only reasonable response to God's love for us?

Paul answers that in the very next verse, and this should be our greatest hope and prayer for our children if we're convinced of the veracity of God's storyline: "Therefore, I urge you, brothers, in view of God's mercy, to offer your bodies as living sacrifices, holy and pleasing to God—this is your spiritual act of worship" (Romans 12:1).

Telling the End of the Story

A life of worship is the only response available to all who truly understand what God has done for us. And the only life we have to give in worship is our own—dead to self and alive to God's bidding.

To do so, we'll have to leave the world's storyline far behind and have our minds thoroughly changed. It's the only way we'll know what God is calling us to do: "Do not conform any longer to the pattern of this world, but be transformed by the renewing of your mind. Then you will be able to test and approve what God's will is—his good, pleasing and perfect will" (Romans 12:2).

If you keep reading in Romans 12, you'll see what this life of worship looks like. Our calling   and that of our families—is to be exactly who God made us to be, disappearing into the body of Christ as we selflessly serve each other with the unique gifts God has given to us.

That's our calling. That's what we hope our kids will see us trying to live out in our everyday adventures at home, in our communities, and especially in our local churches. That's the mantle we hope they'll take up and carry into the next generation.

But it's not the end of the story. It's not the final hope. Our path of worshiping the King leads to God's throne room, to a conclusion that will never end and a finale that's worth fighting for against our own flesh, the world, and even against the Devil.

It is this moment:

Then I saw a new heaven and a new earth, for the first heaven and the first earth had passed away, and there was no longer any sea. I saw the Holy City, the new Jerusalem, coming down out of heaven from God, prepared as a bride beautifully dressed for her husband. And I heard a loud voice from the throne saying, "Now the dwelling of God is with men, and he will live with them. They will be his people, and God himself will be with them and be their God. He will wipe every tear from their eyes. There will be no more death or mourning or crying or pain, for the old order of things has passed away." (Revelation 21:1-4)

Does your family talk about heaven? Do you spend time together wondering out loud what it will be like? Do you ever discuss as a family all of the ways it will eclipse our present, often painful realities? Do your kids know that your greatest hope is to be with God forever in heaven? (*Is* that your greatest hope?) Have you taken the time to begin setting your minds and hope there, as described in the first verses of Colossians 3?

That hope in the endless end of our story is what God means to motivate us—and our kids—to attempt great things for him and keep us going on those dark nights. That hope is what God means to propel us past our selves and the lure of the world's easy answers and headlong toward the prize. It's the hope found in salvation and based on God's grace to us, as described in this paragraph from Titus 2:

For the grace of God that brings salvation has appeared to all men. It teaches us to say "No" to ungodliness and worldly passions, and to live self-controlled, upright and godly lives in this present age, while we wait for the blessed hope—the glori-

ous appearing of our great God and Savior, Jesus
Christ, who gave himself for us to redeem us from
all wickedness and to purify for himself a people
that are his very own, eager to do what is good.
(11-14)

What more could we want for our children—and theirs—
than to say no to worldly passions, to live self-controlled lives,
and to be eager to do good as the people of God?

Let's keep telling them the story. It's not a fairy tale. It's
not make-believe.

It's the story of the real world as God has made it—and
it's the one we pray our kids will live in every day.

Finally, before you close this book, ask yourself these questions:

1. After reading this chapter, what would you say are
    your greatest hopes for your children over the course
    of their lives? What do you believe they would say are
    your greatest hopes for them?

2. How is your ultimate hope—living forever with God
    in eternity—reflected in your choices and attitudes on
    a day-to-day basis in your home?

3. How is your commitment to the reality of God's
    storyline reflected in the risks you encourage your
    kids to take or the future plans you suggest they
    consider?

143

The Wisdom On...series is designed to help your teenagers apply biblical wisdom to their everyday lives. They'll find case studies, personal inventories, interactive activities, and helpful insights from the book of Proverbs, which will show them what wise living looks like.

Wisdom On...Friends, Dating, and Relationships
978-0-310-27927-3

Wisdom On...Getting Along with Parents
978-0-310-27929-7

Wisdom On...Growing in Christ
978-0-310-27932-7

Wisdom On...Making Good Decisions
978-0-310-27926-6

Wisdom On...Music, Movies, and Television
978-0-310-27931-0

Wisdom On...Time & Money
978-0-310-27928-0

Mark Matlock
Retail $9.99 ea.